The Net-Works Guide to

Internet Scams

What to be afraid of
in Cyberspace

Bryan H. Joyce

NET-WORKS

PO BOX 200
Harrogate
HG1 2YR
England

www.net-works.co.uk
Email: sales@net-works.co.uk
Fax: +44 (0) 1423 526035

Net.Works is an imprint of Take That Ltd

ISBN: 1-873668-94-5

10 9 8 7 6 5 4 3 2 1

Printed and bound in The United Kingdom.

Contents

Introduction 5

1. Carders 8

2. Chippers 13

3. Crackers 16

4. Pirates and Forgers 25

5. Hackers 30

6. Phreaks 52

7. Info Junkies 61

8. Newsgroup Scams 65

9. Virus Vandalism 76

10. Protecting Your Information 87

11. Improve Your Onlline Security 103

Last Word 114

Appendix A: Internet Scammer Jargon 116

Appendix B: Scammer/Anti-scammer Resources .121

Dedications & Credits

This work is dedicated to my friend and erstwhile mentor John Lockhart who phoned me in 1988...
"Would you be interested in coming down to our training centre and learning a bit about computers?"
Little did he realise just what he was starting...

Some of the people mentioned below are personal friends or relatives. Sharing lives with them has greatly enriched my own. Thanks for all the encouragement! Others have directly or indirectly provided me with information without which this work would never have been created. To these beautiful people, this work is dedicated. May they live *long* and prosper...

Arthur Gibbson, Beaky (the lovely Sue), Bit (you still owe me a tenner), Bryan Devonish, Bryan Joyce (the original one), Christopher Joyce, Cressida, Dave-Allen Raeburn, Dave - Burns, Fiona McLellan, Firebird, Fliss, Graham Halls, Jack Wraith, Jack Thompson, Jade McLellan (a big trouble maker in a small package), Jamie Devonish, John Lockhart (a cheeky bleepard), John Rampling (yes, I know who you are - hehe), Lauren Stephens, Maggie Joyce (both of them), Henry Schwan, Mitch, Michael S. Hart, Irene Spence, Nemisis, Nonesuch (still owes me a drink), Paul Bocij, Ragnar The Scottish Terrier (Hairy Breeks), Ricky McDade, Steven McLellan and the one known only as Harry.

If anybody wants to get in contact with me to praise, flame or indeed for any reason at all, please send a stamped self-addressed email to...

datajunkie@bigfoot.com

If you *do not* wish your correspondence to be quoted in any possible future works *please* say so. A follow up to *Internet Scams* is not planned as yet, but if this volume is well received, and a follow up demanded, I'll see what I can do. Until then, don't get caught doing anything I wouldn't do...

Introduction

"..And yet his crime was committed more in thoughtlessness than deliberate depravity..."
- A Connecticut Yankee, Mark Twain

Exploitation is ubiquitous these days. Stores take advantage of us. Banks rip us off. Day to day corruptions are everywhere. No one knows who the real crooks are anymore.

Sometimes the exploitation is for personal gain. Other times it's the pastime of the bored and the lazy - the quick buck merchants. Sometimes it is done out of spite and sometimes it is done out of fun. No matter what the motive, in cyberspace, exploitation is a real growth industry.You're about to discover things you've never dreamt about on a bumblebee trip through cyberspace. It will include visits to some *very* dark places; places of profanity and good old-fashioned vulgarity.

This is a book written by an adult for other adults and as such deals with adult issues. It is not for the faint hearted. If this doesn't sound too good to you then please stop reading right now! Close the book and put it in the bin or, what would be better, give it away to someone who would appreciate it.

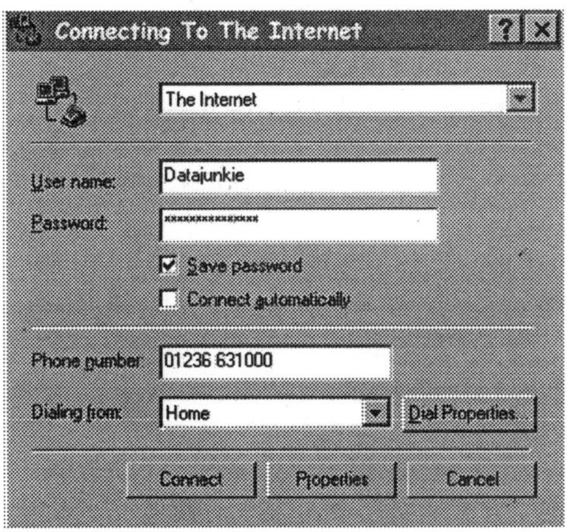

Still here? Good, 'cause you are also going to have a *lot* of fun! During the research for this book, I had the chance to meet a lot of rather colourful, unusual, gifted and fun people. Surprised? Fun people? You thought of the hacker (and their relatives) as bad guys? Whilst this can indeed be the case, in the words of the song, *it ain't necessarily so...*

Cracks in Cyberspace

So what actually is 'cyberspace'? Well, it doesn't really exist. It is an abstract concept. To paraphrase the words of another song, *"It's everywhere and nowhere baby"*.

When you make a phone call, you're dealing with cyberspace. When you talk, you're not aware of the miles upon miles of cables, relays, logic gates and other electronic equipment. To you, the user, the person on the other end of the line seems to be hovering just out of sight somewhere inside the same room. That unknown place - where the phone call happens - is *cyberspace*.

It is a place where dreams and nightmares happen. It is never still. A mysterious infinity. A dynamic system of near organic augmentation and a *Deoxyribonucleic Acid* of complexity.

Virtual identities, spiders and (ro)bots crawl between the flow of faxes, emails, video, sound and other forms of data. A place where acronyms dominate and data is everything. Amongst the data are flaws and cracks in the system. Imperfections explored and exploited by the information junkies, hackers, crackers, pirates and '*darker*' entities.

If you are going to travel there alone, you better be well *tooled* up.

Before we get properly started, I would like to say that I do not acknowledge, judge, condemn or condone anything that is in this volume as good/bad or even worthwhile. It does, however, make interesting reading.

You can, and probably will, make your own mind up about the morality of it all. I might agree/disagree with *some* of the views aired, but to preserve an appearance of impartiality I'm not going to say anything about them except in the very odd occasion. Where views are mine, I will clearly say so.

It is only possible to protect yourself from a Cyber-Scammer or Cyber-Exploiter if you know how their minds work. Indeed, computer security consultants usually start off either as hackers, crackers or information junkies.

The information gathered in this exertion took a long time to accumulate from thousands of sources (a lot of which I no longer have access to) and personal experiences of myself, friends and other parties.

Before you ask, I do *not* claim to be a hacker, cracker or their brethren or *claim* to have ever applied techniques in this field or related activities. I do *not* claim anything. I will however admit to being an obsessively interested party, an information junkie, systems addict and right *Dilbert* if ever there was one.

Hardened hackers use *LINUX/UNIX* (though not as much as they used to). But there is practically zero in this volume about these operating systems, primarily because there has been such a massive amount of stuff already written on the subject. And secondarily, such information is usually of a very technical nature and therefore only of interest to hard-boiled hackers - It would bore the casual reader, if not to death, certainly to sleep. So, nearly all the information contained in this work pertains to an *IBM PC* or compatible running *Microsoft DOS* and/or *Windows.*

A lot of names and nicknames referred to in this volume have been changed to protect the guilty, as well as the innocent. Events have been edited or paraphrased *only* to enhance clarity and readability. I've tried to leave as much as possible untouched.

Everything else is provided *As Is.* No warranties are offered or implied. Batteries are *not* included.

Chapter One

Carders

"...the cards had been stacked against her from the beginning..."
- Song of the Lark, Willa Cather

In a store or restaurant your credit/debit card number is in danger of being copied by the sales staff or discovered later on amongst the refuse.

When ordering products through the post you run the risk of your mail being intercepted and opened. You may even have seen requests for magazine subscriptions that ask you to put your credit card details on the back of a postcard. Yeah, great idea! Like, everyone knows that *all* postal workers are *100%* honest... And then, on top of that, you have the same risk as in a shop with the sales staff copying your details for their own use.

Whilst on the telephone there is the same danger plus the added threat of a crooked engineer/operator listening in or recording your details – yes, it does happen! Call centres are so busy that the operators can (and sometimes do) write down hefty lists of card numbers without anyone noticing.

The cyber way of getting hold of your card details is usually via a website. The Scammer sets up an e-commerce site with an automated mail form to record the card details. They offer a product at amazing prices and entice you to enter your card details. Obviously the product does not exist and the website will very soon disappear. And there are ways and means of hiding the location of such sites so they cannot be checked easily.

The victim would have been unlucky to find the site to start with. They may have been drawn in by plausible recommendations about the company in a *forum* or *newsgroup* or read false details submitted to a search engine.

The victim eagerly enters their card details into the mail form and clicks on 'submit'. If the Scammer is clever an error message comes up saying that the victim is unable to order this item online because of a server/script error. They are then told to try again another time and that if the error keeps re-occurring to report the matter to the company webmaster. Naturally the Scammer will have a fake email address for the Webmaster. This will be an address that looks very like a real company only spelt differently; for example, they might use a name like **www.amason.com** hoping the victim will mistake it for **www.amazon.com.**

The more-careful Scammers will go to lengths to hide the website's address by using the numerical *Internet Protocol* (*IP)* address instead of the text based *Universal Resource Locator* (*URL)*. The advantage of this is that if the victim suspects something is amiss then they won't know what *Internet Service Provider* (*ISP)* to complain to as all you would see is something like this **207.21.195.119.** To complicate things further, the Scammer could also convert the *IP* address into another number base. This number will work just as well as the normal *URL* address or an *IP* address, but is much more confusing to the average user who will not know how to convert it. And if that didn't complicate matters enough, the logon *IP* address of a Scammer can be *spoofed* (faked) to make it even harder to trace them.

An alternative way for the Scammer to get your card details is to target a legitimate site. They hack into it and leave a *bot* (software web robot - sometimes known as a *spider*) that sends them copies of all transactions to a safe email address.

Rumour

Rumour has it that a lot of the stronger pornographic sites are run by 'the mob' (particularly those of the nastier type) or 'Mafioso' of various countries. If you are dim enough to use your card to register or subscribe to one of these sites you can bet your bottom dollar that they will screw more money out of you that you have agreed upon and you won't see it ever again.

Let the Spending Begin...

So, 'they' have got your card number and expiry date. What do they do with it?

One of the common practices is to post details of the card in a newsgroup (sometimes *after* using it to the maximum limit) so that they can be used by anyone. You can imagine the results?

First the Scammer will get further details by phoning the card owner up and pretending to be the credit card company running a security check. Using carefully chosen dialog, they will get the victim's security details such as password, mother's maiden name, date of birth and address etc. You would be amazed at just how much sensitive information you can get out of people just by sounding official, polite and talking jargon.

Next they will phone the credit company (using the security details they've gained from you) to find out how much credit is left on the card. Finally, the spending begins....

If the Scammer is good at forging signatures, they might go on a high street spending spree working in a gang and moving from town to town. Alternatively, they can secure the use of a safe address and order items on the card that can be delivered by next day delivery and will be easy to re-sell. If a safe house is not available, the Scammer will pick someone out of the phonebook and have the stuff delivered to his or her house. They will then turn up at their door asking if a package has been delivered to this address by accident. Sometimes they will even phone ahead and warn the legitimate house owner that some items have accidentally been sent to their address and asking that the parcel be looked after until they can come round and collect it. Naturally, the Scammer needs to be very cool when they come around to collect the booty and it pays to have charisma and look attractive.

The victim will know nothing of these goings on until they either get their statement or try to use the card again only to discover that its limit has already been reached.

It's not just credit/debit cards that are scammed. Any card is at risk: store cards, loyalty cards, club cards, library cards and electricity cards.

Have Software, Can Scam

There is a piece of software in cyberspace called the *Credit Card Number Generator.* It uses a complex algorithm to work out valid card numbers. It is very popular with hackers as they can use it to set up fake temporary accounts with the bigger, more expensive ISPs. The so called free *ISPs* are no good for serious hacking as they insist on the user's *Caller Line Identification* (*CLI*) being sent to the *ISP* which means that there will be a record of the hacker's activities and their phone number.

The bigger *ISPs* who charge monthly rates for access usually aren't interested in the *CLI* so all the hacker needs to do to hide their tracks is to put a short code before the *ISP's* access number and the *CLI* will not be sent. When the credit card details are checked it will be spotted that it is an invalid number, but by then its too late and the hacker will have already disappeared without a trace.

There is also software available for printing cheques. Consider this - the Scammer goes to an Internet auction and puts something pretty ordinary up for auction, perhaps a novel, at a very low price. You see the novel and bid pennies. You win and send the cheque off.

The Scammer feeds the cheque details into the software and prints out a new cheque, which he fills in for a large amount. They would still need to forge a signature and set up a bank account in a fake name, but that isn't all that difficult. This sort of thing actually goes on, though it is not widespread (yet).

Big Bank, Small WAN

One of the biggest exploitations in carding occurred quite a long time ago. It was in London shortly after the introduction of the *Automatic Teller Machine (ATM).*

Employees of the banking system quickly discovered some interesting facts about their new automated money dispenser:

Firstly, the banks were not all connected together. They were grouped into rather large *Wide Area Networks (WANs)*.

Secondly, the more banks in the area the smaller the *WAN's* physical distance across.

Thirdly, when money was drawn out of a bank account, the transaction was only recorded throughout the bank's *WAN*.

Fourthly, the *WANs* only connected up with the mainframe a few times each day. Details of transactions were then sent from the mainframe out to the other *WANs* for updating.

All the exploiter needed was the location of the *WAN* areas. They got it. Someone in the banking system blabbed. Armed with this knowledge, the Scammer started by opening a new bank account in a false name and depositing a hundred pounds.

One hundred pounds was the maximum that the customer was allowed to withdraw in one day. After the account became functional, the Scammer went to the bank and drew out their one hundred pounds. They then got on a tube train and travelled to the next *WAN* zone where the computer system had not yet been updated and drew another one hundred pounds out of the account.

After an afternoon spent travelling from one *WAN* to the next, the Scammer had accumulated quite a tidy sum.

Chapter 2

Chippers

"Everybody says I'm a chip off the old block..."
- Anne Of Avonlea, Lucy Maud Montgomery

Chipping is the art of removing Read Only Memory chips (ROMs) from hardware devices and replacing them with an Erasable Programmable Read Only Memory chip (EPROM) that has had the ROM's code first altered and then copied on to it.

To re-code chips the Scammer uses a piece of hardware called an *EPROM* burner (sometimes know as an *EPROM* blower).

The *EPROM* burner is just a box with a socket on it in which the blank *EPROM* or *ROM* is placed. A cable connects the box to a *PC*. In use, the burner will upload the code from the *ROM* onto the PC where it can be altered using algorithms downloaded from 'Chipping' sites on the Internet. The new code is then downloaded onto a new *EPROM* and the chip put back in the hardware from which it originated.

Another method is to use a *Programmable Interrupt Controller (PIC)*. Unlike an *EPROM*, which is just a place in which to store a piece of code, a *PIC* is directly programmable and can even contain its own memory. It is capable of running its own programs independently - very like a miniature computer. The easiest place to pick up a *PIC* is on the Net, where you will also find tips and techniques being passed between newsgroups.

A popular, harmless pastime at the moment is the chipping of Furby's in order to get them to swear back at you. But, there is a darker side...

A PIC can also be used in a bomb timing mechanism. Its use, however, is very complex, expensive and therefore limited to professional terrorists.

> **Rumour**
>
> The Australian underground were the first Scammers to offer chipped phones to the public.

These days, it is not unusual to buy items such as TVs and VCRs, which have the facility to use a PIN number to protect the device from unwanted users. Chippers, though, can alter stolen hardware so that it can be used without the PIN. Indeed, just about anything with a *ROM* or *EPROM* in it can be chipped. For example, if the Scammer has the ability, they could change the text in the screens of the menu in the *On Screen Display* (*OSD*) of a video recorder. It is within reasonable speculation that they could also add a virus type of code to it to stop it working after a certain date.

Mobile phones can be chipped (and often are). The *'Pay As You Go'* types of services are popular targets. The codes on the phone's chips are set so that when the phone is switched off the credit available is lost. On switching back on, the credit limit is automatically returned to their pre-set amount. Obviously the phones can be used as much as the Scammer wants as when they run out of credit the Scammer just turns the phone off and back on again. Phones that have already been chipped are readily for sale around pubs, clubs and markets.

At the moment, a hardware-programming device can be bought on the Internet for a few hundred pounds that claims to be able to chip any type of *GSM* mobile phone. I suspect this to be a scam in itself, but I'm not sure because I know of a hacking group who did *actually* build such a device in 2000.

Another popular target for the chippers are games machines such as the *PlayStation* that has its forgery detector chip altered so that illicit copies of games will work on it. Also DVDs can be chipped to accept disks from other world zones (where the film distributor is trying to control the release dates or price of a particular film).

Spot the Hoax

"As many of you know, each year the Internet must be shut down for 24 hours in order to allow us to clean it. The cleaning process,

which eliminates dead email and inactive ftp, www and gopher sites, allows for a better working and faster Internet.

This year, the cleaning process will take place from 12:01 a.m.. GMT on February 27 until 12:01 a.m. GMT on February 28 (the time least likely to interfere with ongoing work). During that 24-hour period, five powerful Internet search engines situated around the world will search the Internet and delete any data that they find.

In order to protect your valuable data from deletion we ask that you do the following:

1. *Disconnect all terminals and local area Networks from their Internet connections.*
2. *Shut down all Internet servers, or disconnect them from the Internet.*
3. *Disconnect all disks and hard drives from any connections to the Internet.*
4. *Refrain from connecting any computer to the Internet in any way.*

We understand the inconvenience that this may cause some Internet users, and we apologize. However, we are certain that any inconveniences will be more than made up for by the increased speed and efficiency of the Internet, once it has been cleared of electronic flotsam and jetsam. We thank you for your cooperation".

Email of unknown origin

Chapter Three

Crackers

"...he discovered that he was hungry and the crackers and cheese he had provided for the Journey had all been eaten..."
- The Marvellous Land of Oz, L. Frank Baum

To the Cyber-Scammer, cracking is an art form. This is when copyright protection code segments in retail software are removed (ripped) or altered, where new routines are added, and sometimes where the original code is improved.

Crackers (and hackers) are often forced by necessity to learn their craft. Say a particular software tool may be needed that either does not exist or is not flexible enough. Then it is usually a lot easier to crack, and adapt, an existing piece of software than it is to create a new application. A danger sign that your kids (for it is often they) are on this road is when they start to muck about with the operating system of their computer. Fiddling and customising components that the manufacturer would rather was left alone (see 'How it all begins' opposite).

A cracker is also a specialised form of computer programmer. Their skills may include the ability to do calculations in hexadecimal (number base 16) and binary (number base 2). A strong understanding of assembler language is a prerequisite.

Carders, chippers, pirates and hackers will all need the services of a cracker at sometime or other. It can be difficult (though rewarding) as a lot of code these days is encrypted or has self-repairing segments.

Software developers are making it harder and harder for the cracker. A practice becoming more and more prevalent these days is for software developers to add code that *looks* like copy protection but is, in fact, a decoy. When this decoy is altered it appears to the Scammer that the software has been cracked when actually something on the sinister side has been set free.

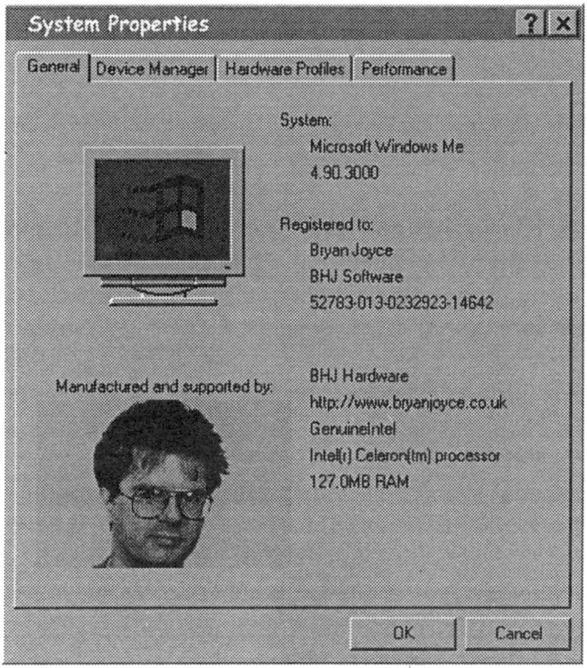

How it all begins

A simple example could be the piece of software that sends a secret email to the software developer's headquarters to report that the individual is using a cracked version of their software. This is not a rumour. I know people to whom this has happened.

Spyware

Software routines that send messages back over the Internet are known as *Spyware* and are becoming more and more ubiquitous in Cyberspace. There are some very popular programs, such as download utilities, that *spy* on the user's activities.

Some crackers can remove the segments of *Spyware* code from software. Other crackers can actually *insert Spyware* into software that was never designed to *spy* on people.

Be warned, anyone who uses cracked software runs the jeopardy of their every move being reported to the Scammer. *Spyware* can keep track of your surfing activities, send copies of all your postings and emails off to a secret address or even examine your hard drive to see what type of files are stored there and send off a report.

Dongles

When a software developer says that their software is uncrackable they are nearly always wrong. One of the hardest copyright protection schemes to circumvent is the hardware device called the *dongle* (great word).

This takes the form of a circuit or EPROM stored inside a small box, which is attached to the computer's Serial, Parallel or Universal Serial Bus (USB) ports. Sometimes it is sealed in a resin-like substance to make it difficult for the cracker to dismantle. The software checks to see if the dongle is there and, if it is not, then the program will not work.

What the talented cracker will do is reverse the process so that the software will only run if the dongle is not present, or they will code their own software that actually simulates a dongle inside the computer's memory.

The Cracking Process

The cracking process is threefold.

- First the cracker has to locate the code segment to be modified.
- Next they have to remove/alter it.
- Finally they write an executable crack or program patch, which will allow the individual to crack their own copy of the target program just by running the program.

Where the target program might be several megabytes in size, the crack/patch is often as small as a few hundred bytes. Generic patch making software exists (often freely available on the Internet) that makes the cracker's job a lot easier.

Typical tools included in the crackers kit might include *Softice* (debugger), *Xtree Gold* (hex editor and other tools), *GREP* (search and replace utility), *Advanced Hex Editor (AXE)*, *Sourcer* (disassembler), *PCWatch* (interrupt monitor), *Tron* (packed

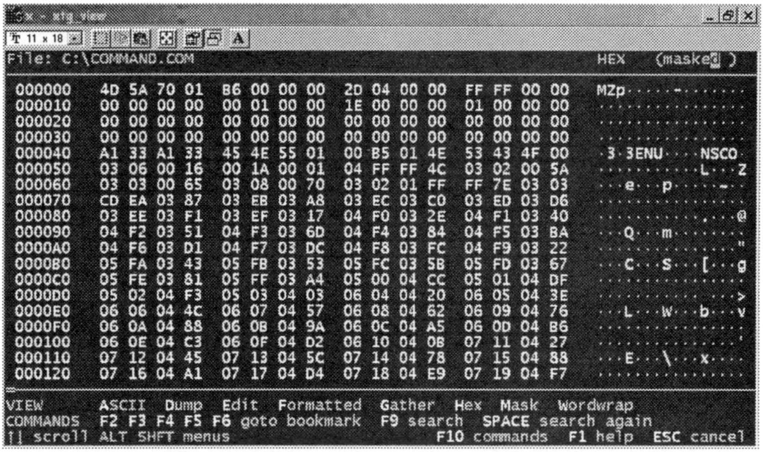

executable unpacker*),* *Boxer (*old but still popular *DOS* text editor*),* *PKware (*archiver*),* *MASM and/*or *TASM (*assembler*),* *Visual BASIC, Delphi* and/or a *C++ Compiler.*

It's not just software cracking tools that are available on the Net. Some of the more useful hardware tools are the software ripper/debugger cartridges and cards that are readily available through mail order or online services.

Legendary devices like *Multiface II*, the *Ultimate Ripper* and the excellent (though no longer manufactured for the *PC*) piece of hardware know as the *Action Replay.*

Some crackers will even go so far as to build their own. These cards can disassemble/edit/load/save a program in memory and/or search for data structures such as music or graphical data as well as many other functions.

One of the first software tools that many a cracker starts off with is provided *free* by *Microsoft.* It is called *DEBUG.*

The Cracking Process

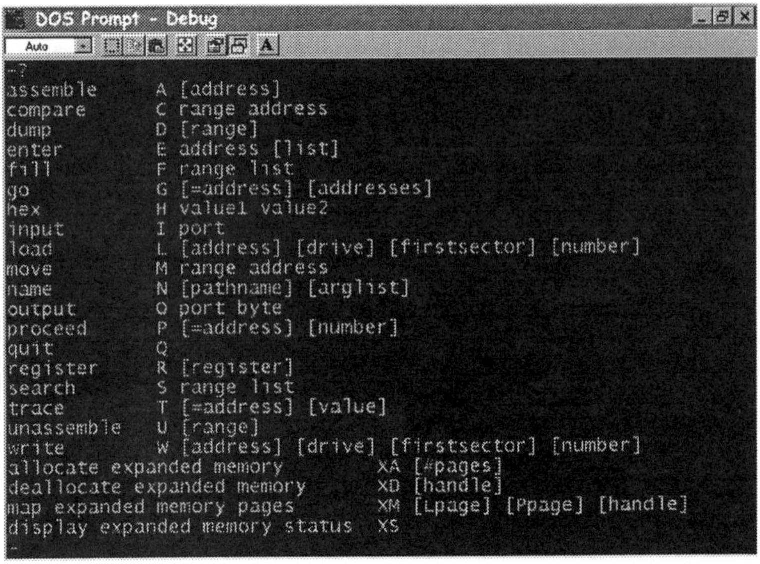

With this utility the cracker can disassemble machine code into assembly op-codes and alter them. *DEBUG* also allows the cracker to build script files that can be used to distribute the crack instructions in a very small automated text file that can be sent by email or downloaded from a website.

A Hobby by any Other Name

In the early days, cracking was a lot easier than it is today. Back at the beginning, the only method of copy protection that really worked was to make the disk 'uncopyable' by burning a microscopic hole in the surface of the 5-inch floppy disk with a laser. This method was abandoned after it was discovered to physically damage floppy disk drives.

Also popular in the early days were protection routines that relied upon *DOS* interrupt vector *13h* (the *h* means hexadecimal). This allowed direct access to the *DOS* disk services functions – but don't worry if this means nothing to you.

Using special software, a disk was created that included one or more unformatted tracks/sectors. Utilising interrupt *13h* the program to be protected would check to see if a particular track/sector was unformatted. If it were unformatted the execution of the program would continue. If not the program terminated.

Disk copy programs in those days could not copy disks with unformatted tracks so the program was effectively copy protected.

Once the crackers found out how interrupt *13h* routines worked, software utilising this technique was easily cracked. It was just a matter of changing a byte or two and the software would no longer check for an unformatted track, but check instead to see if a normal track was there.

The next trick that the software developers tried was to re-program an unused interrupt vector so that it would point to *13h* and use this interrupt instead of *13h,* which made it harder for the cracker to track down as they had to work out what interrupt was being used.

Software developers made such protection a bit harder to crack by the addition of code within the program that created what is known as a *checksum*. This was a hexadecimal number arrived at through a formula operated upon the values of the bytes (or sections of bytes) within the program. If the program was cracked, the *checksum* would change and the program would stop working.

The average cracker barely batted an eyelid as they fixed the *checksums* in their cracked program.

Copy protection routines began to get ever more sophisticated, often using encryption and packing techniques. This did not perturb the cracker who liked the challenge. Protection cracking had become run-of-the-mill. Encryption was what they needed to breath a bit of life back into their hobby!!

In retaliation, the software developers created some rather odd protection routines such as the one implemented in the classic (and brilliant) *Lucas Art* graphical adventure game *The Secret Of Monkey Island*. This used

Rumour

The one time infamous cracker Zippy, of the Atari group The Medway Boys, is reputed to have built one of the first cracking/debugger cartridges. This was then ripped off and marketed by a well known electronics company.

a store of graphic files representing parts of a face to create a random face from three components. The user would then adjust the pictures on a cardboard code wheel until the face matched the one on the screen and type in the character's name as shown on the code wheel. If the correct character's name were entered the game would continue to load. But you couldn't play the game unless you had the stupid cardboard code wheel.

I used to play this game rather a lot and quickly got fed up with the pain in the backside way it had to be loaded using the code wheel. Then one day I had a stroke of luck. I discovered that the coders of *The Secret Of Monkey Island* had left in a macro recording utility (a keystroke/event recorder/player) that had been used to (presumably) test the game. Even better was the fact that you could run macros *before* the code wheel nonsense by simply hitting a particular *F-key* and typing in the macro name.

All that needed to be done was to switch the macro recorder on before entering the characters name and the navigation of the copy protection would be recorded. From then on, when I wanted to play the game, I just ran the macro to get past the copy protection routine. The preposterous cardboard code wheel went straight into the bin.

As mentioned earlier, the cracker usually learns their craft starting off doing small cracks to enhance the operating system of their own computer or the programs they use.

From there they move onto games/utility cracking for which there are readily available tutorials to be found on the World Wide Web. When the cracker develops skill at their craft, they will usually join a cracking group. These groups are strongly competitive. A few of the more legendary groups are *The Legion Of Doom, Automation, The Medway Boys, Chaos* and *Razor.*

These types of groups usually have very outspoken ideas about freedom of speech and encourage the distribution of knowledge on any subjects at all, even if it is potentially harmful, on the grounds that it is for educational purposes only.

The majority advocate the *Try Before You Buy* ethic of shareware and freeware and often include a statement on it with their cracks (well, they would wouldn't they) and some take it all rather seriously...

Chew over these examples.

"Consider the programmers and companies who actually produced the software on this disk. If you would have bought an original version and can afford to do so then BUY it. If you wouldn't have bought it anyway or can't afford to buy it then you are hurting nobody by using the software on this disk. If you use any of this software for business purposes then you should pay for it! Enough moralizing, it's the last thing you want from a pirate :-)"

"It goes without saying, if you use an item of software regularly then when you are no longer a student and have a nice highly-paid job then BUY your own copies of the software (that's what I did). Until then ENJOY and good luck with your studies."

"If I ever find out that anyone has omitted my name from anywhere in these files without my expressed permission, then I will immediately stop doing any updates and I will release your name to as many boards that I can find, urging them to put you on their Black List. I also, will FIND YOU! (I think you can see from the knowledge base contained in this collection that I DO possess the capability! You will wish it were the FEDS and not me!) In other words, be careful who you give this collection to. Of, course there are idiots (probably the same ones who write viruses!) that will misuse this information and kill some people or get themselves & you into a lot of trouble! So keep this treasure chest buried and only dig it up for those that you can TRUST! Also you would be screwing yourself, because I still have all kinds of things that I can put in here for updates, and you will NEVER see them if I quit updating because of some asshole. So think about it. If you WANT the updates (info you would probably have a helluva time finding elsewhere!), then STAY COOL with it."

I don't know about you, but even if he were bluffing, I would think twice before messing with that guy! But, then again, it is possible to intimidate me with a balloon on a stick...

These groups create *CD ROMs* (including their own menu systems) of their patches and cracked software and give it to their trusted contacts and/or pirates to distribute.

While the pirates can make a lot of money out of it, the cracker only has the 'glory' of seeing their nickname on the *CD ROM* menu or by gaining the temporary admiration/respect of their colleagues. The average cracker does it for fun and not monetary remuneration.

Whenever a new piece of software is released onto the market it is a race to see who can crack it first. God help the cracking groups who release a piece of software that has not been properly cracked for they will be the targets of a lot of abuse from other groups.

The cracker usually has an extensive library of computer related books. Their favourite bedtime read is a printed edition of *Ralf Brown's Interrupt List* or a *Windows API* manual.

Crackers are the archetypal computer geeks that gave all computer users the title of nerd. They wear *big* anoraks. *Very big* anoraks...

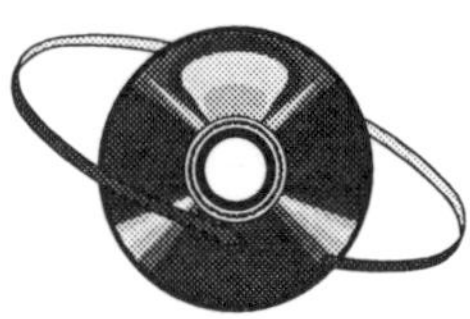

Chapter Four

Pirates and Forgers

"...I believe he'd be a pirate if he dared. There's really something very mysterious about him..."
- Anne Of Avonlea, Lucy Maud Montgomery

The Cyber-Scammer is into forgery and piracy as well. There are colour photocopiers and printers about that cost hundreds of thousands of pounds. With them, money can be copied so accurately that it is never discovered. The money in your pocket may really not be worth the paper it is printed on.

But, that's the obvious scam. What you may not be so aware of is that by using high-power software like CorelDraw and others of the same stable, the talented Scammer can churn out identification documents by the truckload. Birth Certificates, References, CV's, Passports, University/College Qualifications, Vocational Certification and even 100 metres swimming certificates can be forged on a home computer by the average Information Technology student. With the advent of modern, cheap, photo quality laser/inkjet printers, there is really very little that cannot be forged at home.

For example, if the Scammer needed a new identity they would just make themselves a new birth certificate on their *PC* and a fake gas/electricity bill made out to that name. With these two items it is possible to get a library card. With these three items of *ID* it is possible to get a store card. With these four items of *ID* it is now possible to get a bank account and credit cards.

The final item of their new identity would be to get a social security number allocated which happens to be a lot easier than you would expect. No, I'm not telling you how. That would get this book quickly banned and me into a lot of trouble...

In some countries software forgery is big business. Software

Spot The Difference

A forger makes a product that looks like the real thing and passes it off as such. The buyer gets what they think is a proper copy of something like Microsoft Office with the licences, manuals, labels etc at bargain prices. The packaging will even look real (or pretty close). The forged package will sell for slightly less than the real thing.

A pirate, on the other hand, blatantly copies the program, writes a label in felt tip pen and sells it for a nominal sum, usually bundled with loads of other software.

The forger has high overheads, the pirate has very few. A forger makes a high profit, the pirate a smaller one.

disks are bulk copied on professional duplication machines in vast quantities. Labels and packaging are printed to professional standards. They often come complete with authentic looking manuals, licences and other documentation.

More and more software developers are now no longer distributing printed version of the documentation and users have to rely on the 'help files' or online documentation that comes with the software disk. To the forger this is a godsend. It means that there is less to forge!

With some software products costing several hundred pounds (some are over a thousand pounds), there are large profits to be made by the serious forger. Only organised crime syndicates (who are usually into piracy as well) can handle forgery on such a large scale. And if the small-timer starts expanding too much, then it's time for the heavy mob to pay them a visit and perhaps firebomb their working premises/home and rearrange the family pets.

Popular selling places for the *big timers* are the Sunday markets and car boot sales. Glasgow's infamous *Barras* market is raided every few months by forces acting on behalf or with the *Federation Against Software Theft* (*FAST*).

Forgers can go to jail and/or face hefty fines for breach of copyright. Those who are not forgers, but *just* pirates, usually get away with a much lesser fine and having their equipment seized.

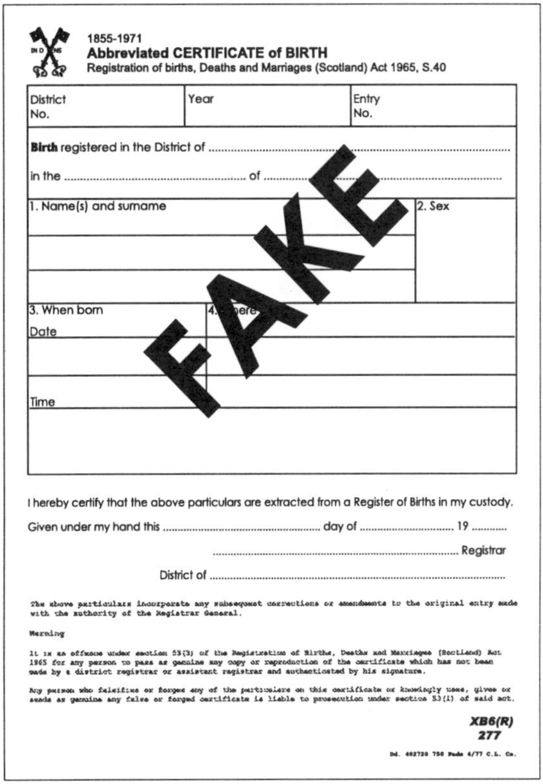
1855-1971
Abbreviated CERTIFICATE of BIRTH
Registration of births, Deaths and Marriages (Scotland) Act 1965, S.40

District No. | Year | Entry No.

Birth registered in the District of ....

in the .... of ....

1. Name(s) and surname | 2. Sex

3. When born | 4. Where

Date

Time

I hereby certify that the above particulars are extracted from a Register of Births in my custody.

Given under my hand this .... day of .... 19 ....

.... Registrar

District of ....

The above particulars incorporate any subsequent corrections or amendments to the original entry made with the authority of the Registrar General.

Warning

It is an offence under section 53(3) of the Registration of Births, Deaths and Marriages (Scotland) Act 1965 for any person to pass as genuine any copy or reproduction of the certificate which has not been made by a district registrar or assistant registrar and authenticated by his signature.

Any person who falsifies or forges any of the particulars on this certificate or knowingly uses, gives or sends as genuine any false or forged certificate is liable to prosecution under section 53(1) of said act.

XB6(R)
277

Dd. 402720 750 Pads 4/77 C.L. Co.

The reason for this being that the copyright breaches involved are not as straight forward as with straight forgery. A typical pirated disk may have hundreds of copyrighted products on it. Who owns the copyright of various code segments has to be determined before the pirates can be prosecuted. And, consider this, most of the products will have been cracked, and the cracked portions and/or patches are copyright of the *cracker*!

Some *warez* dealers don't charge anything at all for their goods. They just set up a website and let anyone who happens by download anything they want as often as they want. Such websites are usually shutdown again very quickly, but usually reappear again just as quickly.

Pirate Patter

Forged and pirated software are also known as warez.

An increasingly popular means of *small time* software pirating is the mail order *warez* dealer. These people frequent Newsgroups and advertise blatantly that you can, for example, buy a copy of *Microsoft Windows 2007* and *Office 2008* together on one disk for only £5 when they would normally cost several hundred pounds to buy in the shops.

The Scammer will usually post an archive detailing their *warez* for sale in a *binary* Newsgroup and wait for people to start ordering. Inside the archive will be details on how to order and often a legal disclaimer like this one:

> *By responding to this message you do affirm that you are not employed by, acting with or for any Software Company, Law Enforcement Agency or associated with any organisation either public or private intent on the prosecution of those involved in Software Piracy. Any misrepresentation of intent by anyone responding to this message can and will certainly be construed as intent*

Notice the 'legalese' phrasing. Few people know if this type of disclaimer has any validity in a court of law, but no one has heard of a *warez* dealer employing these techniques being prosecuted.

The customers of these dealers are also breaking the copyright law, but are unlikely to risk any form of prosecution unless they are buying for a company.

Tempting, as the above may seem, offers are not always as nice as they apparently appear. Sometimes it's not pirates behind the deal at all, but true Scammers. The chances of the consumer receiving their *warez* are zero.

There is an even rarer Scammer that is a cause for concern – the *Pirate*

Rumour

Profits from big time pirates (although there are a lot of small time pirates about, they rarely make any money at it, that's why they are seldom targeted by the authorities) and forgers are rumoured to be ploughed back into other criminal activities such as drug smuggling and gun running.

Extortionist. In this case, the *warez* are sent to the individual as expected. They are then threatened with violence and/or being reported to the authorities if they do not pay up promptly and order more goods on a regular basis. True *Warez* dealers are always on the lookout for these nastier types, and will warn their customers. Even so, think twice before contacting such people. It really isn't worth the risk.

Value for Money

So how do you know if you are getting value for money? Is there anyway in which you can be sure of a product's origins? Well, put it this way, it has been proven by the powers that be, big time counterfeiters are investing considerable outlays into equipment capable of forging holographic product labels. The results of their experiments are already hitting the streets...

Spot the Hoax

"You must forward this letter to 10 people or your account will be terminated on June 1, 1998. All recipients of this email are being tracked.

When you received this, when you forwarded it, who you forwarded it to, is all on record. We are AOL's most elite hacker group, known as LcW. We have hacked AOL's (easily infiltrated) systems on numerous occasions.

We have shut down AOL keywords, we can kick any AOL Staff member off for 24 hours, we have gained access to Steve Case's account, we have created AOL's most famous hacking programs (Fate X, HaVoK, HeLL RaIsEr, MaGeNtA) and we can certainly get your credit card info.

However, if you send this to 10 people, like you are told, you will escape unharmed. We won't terminate your account and you will be able to continue using AOL.

So if you know what's best for you, you will send this to 10 people as soon as possible. If you think we are bluffing....just wait till June 1, and see if you can logon or not.

Email of unknown origin Sent to AOL Subscribers

Chapter Five

Hackers

"I don't say he's such a bad man as I have fancied — I pray to God he is not. But since we don't exactly know what he is, why not behave as if he MIGHT be bad, simply for your own safety? Don't trust him..."
- Thomas Hardy, Far From The Madding Crowd

Hackers have a bad reputation, which is not always justified. Yes, there are malicious hackers about, but they are usually invisible and very good at hiding their tracks. However, the majority, by far, simply hack for fun. What most people fear is the potential for harm.

The keyword here is *potential.* Hackers have the *potential* to cause just as much (or more) trouble as crackers or information junkies - but they rarely do. In fact, the traditional hacker follows a strict credo of *Look But Don't Touch* methodology. They consider themselves to be explorers of cyberspace. They do *not* want to be noticed. If they hack into a system and do nothing more than look around, they are less likely to be caught and/or locked out of that system. If they were to vandalise/abuse that system the security would be improved to the point where they would not be able to get back in again and would therefore be unable to continue to explore that system.

Don't get me wrong, there are malicious hackers about, but they are few and far between. More trouble has been caused by so called '*script kiddies*' than any hacker.

Hackers often write step-by-step tutorials designed to help the would-be hacker get started. Unfortunately, these tutorials sometimes fall into the hands of young, immature, wannabes who have been christened *script kiddies* by the real hackers. The *script kiddie* lacks the patience, skill, knowledge and intelligence to be a hacker.

Instead they use the hacker's step-by-step instructions to break into systems and do something to let the world know that they've been there. This behaviour is the cyber equivalent of spray painting initials on a wall or defacing a public callbox. They want to be noticed. They want to be admired by their peers, and they think the best way to do that is by vandalising the computer system that they have violated. Fortunately, *script kiddies* usually grow out of it quickly or learn the hard way that such behaviour is not cool.

Spotting a Hacker

Ask anyone in the street to give you a psychological profile of a typical hacker (or cyber geek in general) and they will probably give you a list that contains elements from the following.

1) Male

This is increasingly no longer found to be the case. Women have infiltrated cyberspace and they love it! Nowadays there are a lot of female hackers about. They are just as prone to open mindedness, eccentric behaviour and a weird sense of humour as their male counterpart. Indeed, male hackers love them for it and lavish upon them a *great* deal of attention.

In days gone by, women just did not frequent cyberspace at all. I never bumped into any in all the years I spent hanging about *Bulletin Boards* (the predecessor of the Internet).

Not so these days. In fact, they are taking over. They have got their own chat rooms, Newsgroups, websites and even a female-only *ISP*.

2) 14 – 25 years old

Wrong again! The modern hacker can be any age. What do you think happened to all the hackers from the *80's*? They have very probably ended up as Network administrators or proprietors of their own information technology related business, but they keep on hacking nevertheless. There are also pensioners about who love nothing better than to break into some cyber place that they know they should not be in and enjoy the challenge of searching for forbidden knowledge.

I personally know a 50 year-old, female, high school teacher who is an active (and rather good) hacker. She also claims, publicly, to no longer indulge in these practices. Huh, and the other one has got bells on it...

4) Socially inept

This one is way off! Hackers, and their ilk, just love to party! Most like alcohol, coffee and cigarettes *a lot.* They also like tattoos and body piercings as much as any other kind of rebellious personality.

5) Underachiever at school

Whilst this seems to be true a lot of the time (it was with me), many hackers come from the other end of the spectrum, having achieved straight 'A's at school and gone on to University.

6) Above average intelligence

To be a successful hacker (or indeed cracker) you *must* have an understanding of the techniques of problem solving and the application of these methods to new (and sometimes abstract) concepts. So, you could, indeed, say hackers must be intelligent (though doesn't always have the maturity to go with it). Learning to hack properly is also a long, hard slog. Sooner or later all hackers have to bow down to the methodologies of a structured (self) education or eventually give up the hobby altogether. Sure, the *School Of Life* can be effective, but 'real' education is quicker and more effective.

Script kiddies can be intelligent too, its just that they the lack motivation to learn the hard way.

7) Unsuccessful with the opposite sex

Untrue. They are just as likely to be good family men/woman as anyone else (only with more computers).

8) Unable to sustain long-term relationships

In today's modern society, few people are interested in sustaining a long-term relationship and the hacker isn't any different in this aspect to anyone else. However, I do know an ex-hacker who has three kids. He and his wife have their own *PCs*, which they have networked up to the kid's machines so that they can keep an eye on them. They aren't particularly wealthy and live in a council house (admittedly a rather large one). They just have different priorities to you and me (well, you anyway).

9) Few interests outside of computers

These days, a computer is a tool for enhancing other hobbies such as databases for collectors and word processors for writers. Hobbyists are swarming to cyberspace.

10) Science fiction fan

Spot on. Hackers are nearly always *Trekkies*.

11) Unable to keep permanent employment

There is an element of truth in this. Hackers, like a lot of supposedly intelligent people, get bored easily. Being stuck in the same old job every day (unless its computer related) is anathema to them.

12) Work shy

No more true than in any other walk of life. In fact, in the field of information technology, (coding in particular) the hacker is likely to be a workaholic simply because they enjoy it so much. While the legendary millionaire computer whiz kid is getting rarer these days, there are still a lot of highly paid forms of related employment to be found in this area where the cyber workaholics can exploit themselves.

Strange Happenings

So just what am I saying here? The media are wrong? Hackers are really good guys? A tiny misguided minority giving them all a bad name? No, not quite...

There are a lot of unusual goings on that the man in the street will never get to know about. They are either not newsworthy or so unbelievable as to be unprintable. The rumours don't help. Neither do words like, *"potential"* and *"what would happen if?"*

The word entropy is the hackers friend. Entropy is an enveloping word used to describe the tendencies of all systems to naturally fall into disrepair. Hackers seek out entropy. Encourage it and exploit it. The biggest hackers of the lot are people who work in a position of trust within the system.

Technicians who work for ISP's allowing privileges for their friends. For example, most ISP's will give away perhaps 10 to 30 megabytes in free webspace. If you know any technicians they can tell you how to get as much room as you want and not have anyone know about it. A hacker will often figure this out themselves, but why should they if their pal *"Big Tam"* the technician will do it for a couple of pints?

This is a real example. It does happen. And the Internet is the ideal place in which to swap information. *"Don't tell anyone else this, but I got a pal who works for Viniculum.net and he says..."* This is the tip of the iceberg. Consider that the Internet is a *facilitator* of all forms of hacking. The ultimate way to avoid being caught with sensitive information is to put it in the public domain.

Cable, TV and ISP companies are particular targets. It is not unusual for disgruntled employees to set up a website that blatantly advertises and sells off (on rare occasions they give it away) the company secrets. You can actually buy decoding equipment online that has been home built by ex-technicians as revenge for being badly treated by their former companies. Just think. To be able to get all the cable channels that you want forever for a one-off payment? Bliss!

Still this is small time. Some hackers have tremendous powers and end up, though sheer frustration, making themselves infamous. In 2000 a hacker spotted several gaping security holes in a famous online (encrypted) banking system. He informed the company who did nothing about it. In a mind bogglingly stupid move, he decided to help the customers out by hacking the website, removing details of tens of thousands of customers' credit card details and putting the details into the public domain. In his eyes, he was doing a public service, but try telling that to the card owners. The powers that be were not amused. He went directly to jail (admittedly not for very long). Did not pass go. Did not collect £200.

Respect

Just think, the second richest man (at the time of writing) in the world, is also the worlds' most well-known cyber geek. You would think that he would be a good role model and perhaps even hero to hackers? Wrong!

For some strange reason there are two things that nearly all hackers (and crackers) abhor. One is the Microsoft Corporation and the other is the ISP America On Line (AOL). Both are successful international companies with a truly massive customer base. When you consider the scale of their investments, they provide popular reliable products at reasonable prices.

But the average hacker can't understand why Microsoft would want to market an operating system when they could give it away free like LINUX.

AOL provides a secure and user-friendly interface to the Internet. Hackers do not like this. They need complexity so that they can look for cracks.

Generally, if something is doing what it is supposed to be doing, works efficiently and its developers have the audacity to expect a return on their investment, the hackers ain't happy about it. Hackers are strange people...

Yet, we are still talking small time here. *Mafia* type organisations employ hackers. So do *MI5*, the *FBI,* etc. It is rumoured that organisations with aims as diverse as saving the world, through to terrorism have been known to secure the services of hackers.

What do these hackers get up to? Well, because of their very nature, it is very hard to confirm the rumours. But here are a couple of examples...

Quite a while ago, I was working with this young man who claimed to have been one of the designers who coded the software in use at a well-known airport. He claimed that he was extremely underpaid and did a favour for a certain notorious group of people. He installed a backdoor (a secret way in) to the flight software. Once in, a password would activate a process where variables were switched and aircraft details for taking off and landing would be all mucked up creating chaos.

Now I am not familiar with aircraft software and personally think that this guy was talking a load of tripe (he was too young to have been there for a start). But the cause for concern is that such a thing *is* possible. If an individual is capable of such complex coding then they are also capable not only of doing this, but hiding it.

A few years back, a casual acquaintance of mine (uses the nickname of Dirty Harry) told me about a hack that he had done (and claimed to be still doing the last time I heard from him) to a mail order company. You know the type I mean? The ones where they send out a thousand page catalogue of clothing, furniture, hi-fi etc and allow you to pay for it over 20, 40 or even a hundred weeks. Dirty Harry claimed to have perfected a technique where he can order what he wants. Then after receiving delivery, he performs a bit of hackery pokery and hey presto! The bill has been mysteriously settled in full.

On questioning, Dirty Harry revealed that it was not really his hack. Someone who he had become rather friendly with on the Internet (who he referred to as an Internet phantom) had supplied the information. I was given enough details to have a go at hacking it myself (which I would never do), but Dirty Harry refused point blank to give out the logon details and password. He said that this Internet phantom had given him the info on the understanding that it not be passed on to anyone at all. I pressed him on this matter, but he would not budge. I don't know if he was scared of this so-called Internet phantom or just refusing to cooperate due to it being a load of prevarication. In retrospect, I have come to the most likely conclusion that he refused to elaborate simply in order to annoy me.

Anyway, I had the phone number of the (supposed) company's mainframe. And curiosity being the nature of the beast...

I did a bit of information gathering and discovered that this mainframe number was close enough to their order line phone number to be discovered by using a War Dialler (see the chapter on Phreaks). I fired up my terminal program in standard ANSI mode and tried to connect to the mainframe.

The tones coming from my modem indicated that there was

either a fax or a computer at the other end of the phone line. And then it connected to something that looked like the logon screen of a typical *Packet Assembler Disassembler* (*PAD*), which is an older style of network access point. The HELP command did nothing. Neither did sending escapes, returns or control codes. I suspect that it may have connected to a multiplexer type device (a hardware anti-hacking device). After a couple of minutes of fruitless command attempts came the ubiquitous NO CARRIER message, which meant that I had been disconnected. There was no need to go any further. The point had been proved.

During the recounting of this tale to another of my acquaintances (nicknamed Dot), she told me of how, in the early 90's, her mail order catalogue account (a different company) got wiped when the company mainframe hard drive got mysteriously wiped along with the back-ups. All the customers were sent out letters asking them to let the company know how much money they still owed, as they had no records at all regarding several thousand people. Not only did Dot not inform the company about the £700 that she owed, but claimed to me that the accident was not an accident, but someone doing her a favour. Unfortunately, for the sake of this story, it was not a clever hacker, but a disgruntled employee. Like I said earlier, hacking is easy when you are part of the system. It's the outsiders - those Internet Phantoms - who have the *real* talent.

In both these examples, I am left with some small doubts to the credibility. I will never know the truth because both incidents are well within the grounds of reasonable possibility. All they require is for someone within the system in a position where they can look the other way for a moment or give out a key piece of information.

In conclusion, let me list some of the truths about hackers. The *potential* of them. But do not worry about this list too much, although *possible*, most of them will never happen. Well, at least not to you. It's somebody else's problem. But then again..?

- Train crashes can be caused.
- Air crashes can be caused.
- Your identity can be wiped.
- New identities are easier to create than you think.
- No website is unhackable.
- No software is uncrackable.

- There are viruses that cannot be detected.
- Your medical records can be adjusted.
- Your criminal record can be adjusted.
- Online shopping is not safe.
- Everything can be faked.
- Your life can be ruined through the Internet.
- Hackers *are* in the banking system.
- You *are* being watched (and not just by the government).

Data is nothing but raw knowledge. Knowledge is money. Money is power.

The Good Guys

People are being routinely ripped off in cyberspace. Hackers are not always the bad guys, but some of them *really* make up for the rest. And some of them are, just... well... plain... nice...

Take this gem. In 1999 Steve - a disabled friend of mine (cerebral palsy) - had a bit of bad luck. His two loves in life (he lives alone) are his TV and his computer. His TV broke down just after the guarantee expired. For several weeks he moaned and moaned to anyone who would listen about how much he missed it and couldn't buy a new one.

Then one day, a deliveryman turned up with a 28 inch wide-screen TV. Steve refused to sign the delivery note on the grounds that he had not bought it. The deliveryman showed him the delivery note. Steve's details were on it and so was the legend, *"Paid In Full"*. To cut a long story short, Steve would have nothing to do with the thing and insisted that the courier take the damn thing back to the warehouse.

A few weeks went by and Steve got a letter containing a cheque refunding his payment for the TV. Again, Steve would not have anything to do with it. Like most people, he is not particularly honest, but just scared of getting into trouble. Eventually, after a phone call to the company, a visit to the Citizens Advice Bureau and several people nagging him, Steve gave in and cashed the cheque. He bought a nice 22-inch set and had quite a bit left over.

The person who caused this (no clues) did it through a major online electrical retailer. Technically, it was not much of a hack as

there was also a certain degree of Social Engineering involved. Naturally I was requested by the perpetrator not to elaborate further on this matter, *"...or else..."*. And if you think that I'm scared of a vague threat like this, you'd be darned right!
In summation, if it exists as a flow of data it can be hacked.

- ✔ Charities *do* have mysteriously large donations transferred into their accounts from untraceable sources.
- ✔ Patients *are* suddenly and unaccountably moved to the top of NHS waiting lists.
- ✔ Confidential information about murderers, rapists and paedophiles *is* leaked to the media with astonishing regularity.

I consider myself very lucky in that I've knowledge of quite a few particularly interesting people who know other particularly interesting people. Now and then, I have been witness to some pretty *unusual* goings on. Once in a blue moon, I have actually been part of them, but mostly I get to hear things. Privileged information. *Damn* privileged information...

The only way in which to safeguard information is to isolate it. In today's global village this is increasingly difficult. Networking is not just a trend but also a necessity. If a computer is connected to another computer in any manner whatsoever, then it is at risk. If that computer is connected to the Internet, the danger is increased a million fold.

Consider, the really big corporations get hacked all the time. The stronger the need to keep someone out, the more people will try to get in. Attacks on the big boys are measured in tens of *thousands* per year. Nothing is unhackable. Hackers *can* get in. Hackers *will* get in...

Hacktivism

There has been a considerable increase of activist groups utilising hacking techniques to get their messages across. The term *"Hacktivism"* was born as a general reference to anyone who hacks for what they consider to be a higher moral reason such as patriotism or political beliefs.

- A BBC internal communications network was hacked and defaced by the group *Silverlords For The Freedom Of Kashmir*.

- In the Middle East, the website of the Muslim militant group *Hamas* was hacked and links added to hard-core pornographic sites. This happened after *Hamas* took responsibility for a bombing in the Israeli town of Netanya.

- In Israel, popular politician Ariel Sharon's campaign website was hacked and replaced with pro-Palestinian material and a slogan claiming that he was *"The World's Biggest Murderer"*. Sharon went on to win the election by a landslide.

- In 2001, the Punjab Government website was taken over and replaced with a message thanking the Pakistan army for their help in overthrowing the government.

- During the Kargil conflict between India and Pakistan, an Indian army website was hijacked and used to display information on the alleged torture of Kashmiris by the Indian security forces.

- Back in 1998, the website of the Kosovo Information Centre (KIC) was hacked by the Serbian terrorist organisation known as the *Black Hand*. The new homepage proclaimed the KIC to be the *"biggest liars and killers"* in the world.

The year 2001 saw the first true cyber war. It all started when a US spyplane crashed into a Chinese fighter aircraft. The Chinese plane crashed into the sea killing its pilot. The crew of the US plane were held captive by China.

This incarceration of US citizens started off the cyber war. During the 11 days that the airmen were held captive, hundreds of Chinese websites were hacked and defaced with anti-Chinese graffiti.

Chinese hackers immediately responded with tit-for-tat website hacks of their own. In the first week of retaliation, Chinese hackers damaged over 600 websites, mostly with anti-US graffiti, but, on occasion, intentionally destroying data by leaving malicious scripts which would auto-run on rebooting of the systems.

Software engineers on both sides of the war were laughing all the way to the bank as they were called to improve network security at exaggerated costs. Systems were patched extremely quickly and sites considered sensitive were temporarily shut down.

The FBI reported that there was a *"significant amount"* of increased attempts to gain access to official websites such as the CIA, the Pentagon, US Navy and National Security Agency. At one point the White House website was offline for several hours. Spokesmen issued confusing statements to the effect that security *"had not been"* breached, but that the *"attack"* was being investigated.

Within a month of the spyplane incident, US hackers had defaced over 450 websites, whilst the Chinese hackers claimed to have succeeded in over a thousand such attacks.

Also in 2001, a 14 year old boy, after reading a computer magazine article about alleged anti-Semitic websites, claimed to have destroyed an Iraqi government website which contained, what he termed, anti-Israeli lies and propaganda. He further claimed that he had created a virus, which would destroy all Iraqi sites on the Internet.

Despite the Iraqi government stating that this event never occurred, but admitting that they had found (but not activated) a virus sent from the boy in an email attachment, the teenager still managed to achieve hero status. He received considerable media attention and a massive amount of congratulatory mail and phone calls.

Do you think hackers are currently being recruited by the armed forces? And how far off do you think the first war conducted entirely on the Internet may be?

Your First Hack

The word *"Hacking"* is often used as by the media as a catch-all term for anyone using a computer for criminal activity. Programmers, on the other hand, simply use the term to mean rushing a job or creating a temporary solution.

If you change any programme to make it run slightly better, or to customise it beyond the manufacturer's original specifications, you too are a hacker. This includes giving yourself extra lives, ammunition or jumping between levels in computer games. And you don't have to have figured out what to do yourself. If you have read, perhaps on the Internet, that typing 'Rock On' into the dialogue box of *Age of Empires* gives you 1000 more stone, and you do it, you have 'hacked' that game.

These pastimes are a form of legal hacking, which could also be thought of as debugging (a programmer term which means to track down faults and locate areas for 'improvement').

A classic example of an operating system *"tweak"* is changing the 'manufacturer' of you compter. Before you read on, try it for yourself. Locate the system information on your desktop (clue: My Computer>Control Panel>System) and use all the ways you know of to try and change the name and logo of your computer manufacturer – right clicking, Windows Explorer, changing properties, none of them work.

But here's how to do it. Follow these instructions (on your own computer, obviously) and you will perform your first 'hack'*.

** Whilst this 'hack' will work on most computers, it is not guaranteed. The author, TTL and their agents cannot take any responsibility if you freely choose to experiment with it on your own computer.*

1) First create a bitmap graphic approximately 120 pixels by 120; say a picture of your cat.
2) Save it as OEMlogo.bmp.
3) Create a text file containing information similar to this:.
   [general]
   Manufacturer=Your Name
   Model=An Elastic Band Computer
   [Support Information]
   Line2= This is an example

Line3= of the sort of thing
Line4= that can be discovered
Line5= with a bit of thought

4) Save it as OEMinfo.ini.
5) Copy both files into \Windows\System folder overwriting those already present (though you might want to back them up first).
6) Go into the Control Panel and open System and look at your handiwork.

And there you have it, your first hack. A similar process would change the opening screen when Windows is starting. If you put a rude picture on someone else's machine, you are on the road to ruin!

Tools of the Trade

Serious hacking can be achieved using any minimum-specification computer, a bog standard modem and little in the way of software tools. Hacking is all about knowledge and technique.

Nevertheless, good quality hardware and powerful software tools can ease the hackers' task. Amongst these tools are things like *finger clients*, *whois* clients, IP *tracers* and the ubiquitous *port scanner*. The latter looks for ways into computers. The former are detective tools used to track people down. One of the best of such tools is the aptly named Sam Spade. These functions, and others, are often included within the one software tool like the excellent *Netlab*.

Some of the most popular hacking tools have been around for quite a while. Among them are the *ping, Netstat, nbtstat* and the *telnet client* provided free with *Windows*. The later is command-line parser used to negotiate and manipulate within UNIX /LINUX environments without the need of a Graphic User Interface (GUI). It can allow access to places where web browsers cannot reach. The former tools report various statistics such as journey rates for data test packets, which ports are currently active and what they are connected to.

All of these tools are also friendly to people who are trying to track down intruders.

A Typical Hack

So how do they actually perform a hack? How do they get into websites and, once there, what can they do?

Well, believe it or not, if you have got this far in the book, you already have enough knowledge to *"potentially"* perform a website hack; the tools have been mentioned, as have the basic techniques. It is now time to go just a little bit further. And when I say, *"little bit"*, I really do mean it. This section is no more than a general guide to a typical implementation of one methodology. It is a reasonable scenario (if rather simplified) of a website hack. Just enough to give you the flavour of what goes on. All addresses shown are invented except for 0.0.0.0 and 127.0.0.1 which are local addresses and little to do with the Internet other than as an indication of online status.

1) Identifying The Target

The first thing to do is to get the IP address of the target website. The quickest way is to run *netstat* with the -a -n switches. If the hacker got back something like this...

```
Active Connections
Proto   Local Address     Foreign Address   State
TCP     0.0.0.0:5000       0.0.0.0:0        LISTENING
UDP     127.0.0.1:1900    *:*
```

Then the computer is offline.

A typical online report might look something like this...

```
Active Connections

Proto   Local Address     Foreign Address   State
TCP     0.0.0.0:5000       0.0.0.0:0        LISTENING
TCP     113.48.71.23:139   0.0.0.0:0        LISTENING
UDP     127.0.0.1:1900    *:*
UDP     113.48.71.23:137  *:*
UDP     113.48.71.23:138  *:*
```

Notice that ports 5000 and 139 are listening for events. Port 5000 is local and port 139 is connected to the *ISP* main server. If the hacker was connected to a *POP, FTP, HTTP* or any other server, it would also show up in the statistics. If they were to run their web browser, connect to the target website and then run *netstat* again it would also show the IP address of the target.

Armed with this IP address, other tools such as *Sam Spade* or *NetLab* can provide a considerable amount of information about the website, even down to the registered owner details.

2) Safe Attack

The easiest attack would be to simply run a *TelNet* client and try to connect to standard ports (such as the default *Telnet* and *FTP* ports) at the target's IP address. This is unlikely to have much success, but if it does (and it has been known), you are more or less inside.

3) Risky Attack

The other main method is more likely to succeed, but the hacker is much more likely to get caught. The site's IP address is dumped into a port scanner and left to see if it can find any open ports. This type of scanning has a realistic likelihood of setting off an alarm or trace which could get the hacker into trouble. Usually the worst that happens is that their ISP bans them from their network.

The cautious hacker would not consider any form of scanning without first connecting through a proxy server. This type of server can be thought of as a stepping stone towards the target. Any tracing would lead back to the proxy and then back to the hacker. It decreases the likelihood of being traced, but isn't a sure-fire method.

A very cautious hacker would fake his own IP address (*spoof*) or use a proxy and fake his IP address. Neither is of much help if the target is a big company with the time and resources to follow it up. There are no foolproof ways to hide in cyberspace - everything leaves traces - but plenty of ways exist to make it extremely unlikely to ever be traced.

If the port scanner picks up an open port, then the hacker can *TelNet* their way in.

If neither of these basic methods work, the hacker would try mucking about with the likes of FTP clients and (unbelievable as it may sound) sometime even a simple web browser can find a way in.

If these Internet resources result in negative results, it is time to try social engineering the host ISP. Difficult as it may be to believe, armed only with the victim's name, address and postcode, many ISPs will give out passwords and user IDs (which is often just their email address and, as such, can be guessed) on the pretext of the hacker claiming to have lost them. I personally have experience of two ISPs who allow this sort of thing. Thankfully the one that I now use doesn't, which is why I picked it in the first place.

4) What Success Brings

So the hacker is inside the website. What now? Well, not a lot. Vandalism, exploration or the opportunity to play jokes are about the limit. Very often the only reason that the hack was done in the first place is either because someone claimed that it couldn't be done, was a challenge or just for the hell or it. You, on the other hand, as a radical extremist know how to change your system manufacturer's information (see page 42).

So-called black-hat hackers will be looking for things such as credit card details or confidential information. Hacking has become of an increasing interest as a means for activists to get their points across to a larger audience. Extreme political or prejudiced groups are popular targets.

When it comes down to the bare bones of it all, trespassing on a government website in order to draw a pair of glasses on the Prime Minister's photograph is a damn fun thing to do. The hacker enjoys it. Their peers enjoy it. The newspapers enjoy writing about it. And the eyes of every wannabe hacker twinkle with longing.

A certain famous writer of books about the dangers of the Internet was recently on TV claiming that security on the Internet was a joke. He could show *anyone* how to break into *any* website within a couple of minutes. Whilst this exaggerated claim has some basis in fact, his point is valid only if he happens to be about whenever anyone wants to break into a website. Since he is unlikely to be available at the time, it was a particularly pointless claim to make...

The Firewall

Firewalls are a piece of software designed to keep hackers out. *Zonealarm* is a good example (and free for personal use).

After it is installed and configured, a *firewall* is best forgotten about. When I first installed a firewall, I was interested to find out what these attacks were and often used to go to the *IP* address reported as the origin of the attack. Usually there is nothing there as the *IP* address of the intruder is dynamically allocated and will change every time they logon - but sometimes you get a surprise.

An example is when the intruder is running a piece of software known as *ICQ* (*I Seek You*). *ICQ* is one of a group of software tools known as instant messengers. With it you can tell when your friends are online at the same time as you and chat to them in real time. The *ICQ* Network is run by *AOL*.

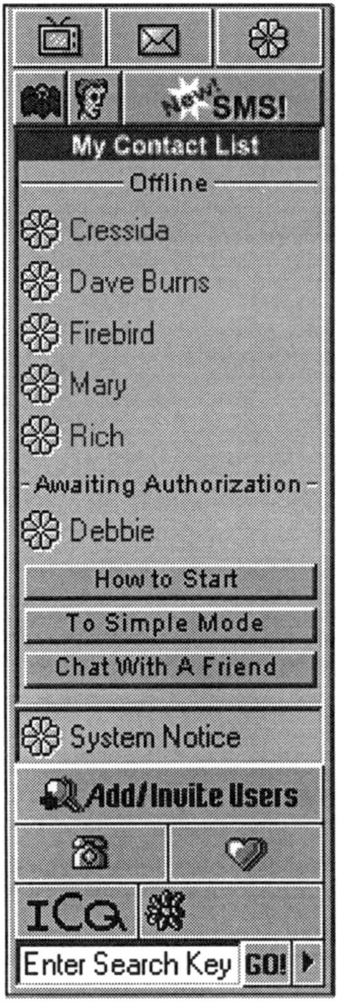

One of *ICQ's* features is that it will (if you wish) allocate the user a small homepage containing the users details so that other users can find out about them. A side effect of this is that the *ICQ* users *IP* address is re-routed to this homepage every time they connect to *ICQ*.

If the person scanning happens to be connected to *ICQ* at the time when they are scanning for open ports, the intruder is easily traced to their *ICQ* homepage and their details discovered.

This *ICQ* homepage has quite a few security flaws in it and thus is reasonably easy for even a hacking beginner or *script kiddie* to use it to exploit the owners' hard drive and do bad things to it.

For example, one of my friends had been surfing for about an hour at his place of employment when suddenly his desktop background picture changed as if by magic to something *very* pornographic.

A few moments later, he received an email.

"Ha ha! You have just been hacked!!!!!"

The email appeared to have been written (and sent from) his own email address. Shortly after this incident he bought and installed a *firewall*.

If you use the Internet and don't have a firewall – think again.

When The FBI Knocks

Ever wondered what happens when a hacker gets caught? Here is a hint. This is what can happen when you are just in the wrong place at the wrong time.

I'm writing this for two reasons:
1) I'm getting tired of explaining it over and over to friends.
2) To make people aware that they're not being paranoid enough. This story should scare you

Those of you who know me know that I am in no way a Script Kiddie. I'm simply a student, in various IT disciplines and programmer who likes to dabble in cryptography, LINUX kernel hacking, data compression, and whatever else the topic of the week happens to be. I also have a short attention span, skipping from project to project, subject to subject. I do not claim to be an expert in any field, but I know my way around.

One Saturday afternoon (Oct. 28, 2000, 4 PM), the FBI let themselves into my dorm (my school gave them the keys), waking me up. They showed me a badge, handed me a warrant, and took me into another room to ask me questions. They had every intention of seizing all my computer hardware before even questioning me, which should worry you greatly.

They initially began asking me if I was a baseball fan, which confused me. After answering with a "no", they explained that I was under investigation for the break in that had occurred the previous day to the Yankees website. I breathed a sigh of relief (my initial reaction was, "Oh shit, someone's pissed about my 30 gigabyte MP3 collection!"), as I figured I could simply explain to them what

Worry Not

When you first install a *firewall* you may be alarmed to discover a large amount of scans being detected and blocked. Not all of these are cyber Scammers. A sizable percentage will be servers trying to re-connect from previous bad disconnects or simply *Spyware* in action.

happened, and they'd leave my stuff alone. I was wrong. The previous day, I was doing my usual routine for a Friday with no class; up at 7 AM, supposed to be catching up with homework. Of course, the whole time, I'd be on Internet Relay Chat (IRC) talking with people. During a conversation about Microsoft's break in, and how the stolen source code would affect things like Wine (a LINUX program), a friend mentioned that www.yankees.com had also just been hacked.

Being the curious individual that I am, I went to the mentioned web page, and discovered that it had, indeed, been cracked (and replaced with a rather amusing picture, and a "Yankees Suck!" banner).

I then began a post-mortem inspection; I always find this to be very interesting, as several friends have basically handed me LINUX boxes (not physically handed, of course), and asked me to rid them of a certain pesky cracker. The last time I did this, I discovered the intruder had gotten in through a (well-known) security hole in LINUX Redhat 6.2.

I first checked port 21 of www.yankees.com, noticing the same security hole that had been exploited in the aforementioned cleanup. That didn't sound right to me; it was www.yankees.com, they had to have better security than that? So, I did a zone transfer of www.yankees.com, and noticed another older www.yankees.com.

Upon going there, I saw what I thought to be the original site, so I figured this whole so called "crack" was simply a redirection of the URL. I checked the version of Bind and did some port scanning, but found nothing worth mentioning.

The next day, I was sitting in a chair in the lounge, with an older FBI agent and another person who had not identified himself (but had a clue about computer stuff). I tried to explain the situation as best as possible; I probably did a horrible job, as I had just woken up (brutal LAN party the night before :) and really didn't remember many of the details. It was just a five minute segment of my previous day, and I had spent much time coding and on IRC.

The FBI started grilling me on IPs; if I had accounts on various machines, etc. At first, I had no idea where they were going with this. I assumed they had firewall logs, and saw many, many connections to my machine, I realized that they were seeing hits from my webpage, which included modified versions of various free software. I answered their questions as best I could, even though I was told I did not have to; I had nothing to hide.

Overall, they were pretty nice. They took three computers, two books (ORA's DNS & Bind, and a book on kernel hacking), and various scraps of papers, which contained jotted down algorithms, code, and other stuff I had written while bored or designing.

They let me go through my notes, and pick out stuff I needed for class; they also (upon my request) let me keep my "junk box" (cardboard box w/ various pieces of hardware), as well as 80 cd-r's, which contained mostly MP3's, (they also made sure that there was no kiddie porn).

As you can see, they really only cared about cracking, which I had nothing to worry about. Unfortunately, they took all my back-ups.

I have not been formally charged yet, nor do I fear I will be. I'm worried most about the data on my drives, which is a combination of source code, various scripts and tweaks I had done to my LINUX Debian boxes over the two years I've been running it, and essential data (email addresses of friends, developers; class projects, some of which I HAVE needed since then; email itself; etc).

This brings me to the whole point of this: you are not being paranoid enough. The FBI managed to get a search warrant based on logs from a firewall, that showed my IP only connecting, not even logging in, hours after news of the cracking had appeared on news sites.

If they can get a search warrant this easily, your data is not safe, sitting on your hard drive. For the past two months I've been living in this dorm, I locked my doors, secured my boxes, and backed up my essential things. I never even imagined the federal government would just let themselves in and take it.

The moral of the story is: encrypting all sessions, is not enough. Nor is making back-ups. Make off-site back-ups. The FBI can arrive at your doorstep, with every intent of taking your precious data, and not returning it for a long, long, loooong time."

Andres Salomon

Chapter Six

Phreaks

"..Indulging our fancy in this freak, we have partly lost the power of restraint and guidance..."
- House of Seven Gables, Nathanial Hawthorne

An American sub-culture began to emerge in the late 60's known as Fone Phreaks. Their purpose in life was to steal phone calls (i.e. make them for free) and to generally explore the telephone system (which was, and still is, the biggest computer system ever built).

Actually *British Fone Phreaks* were at it first but, of course, their *American* counterparts did it bigger. A *phreak* who was to become legendary (known as *Captain Crunch*) discovered that a free whistle given away with *Cap'n'Crunch* breakfast cereal allowed him to make free calls. He did not keep this information to himself, but spread it about.

As a result of the *Captain's* endeavours, *phreaking* became a popular pastime in the *USA*. The phone system was minutely explored and numerous other flaws discovered and ruthlessly exploited. One such flaw was the existence of test lines that allow several people to phone in free of charge and have their own conference. These types of calls became intelligence centres for *phreaks*.

As new techniques were discovered so they were shared amongst the community. One of these techniques was the discovery that a *blue box* could be used to tap into phone lines that were already in use to enjoy listening in to the conversations.

The Blue Box

While it took a bit of knowledge to reap the full rewards of the blue box, anyone who could solder a few bits and pieces together could use it to make free phone calls to anywhere in the world.

All the *blue box* did was emulate the tones used by telephones and other tones used by operators. An extra button emulated a very special tone known as the *phreak* tone - *2600* hertz (or in the *UK 2280* hertz). This tone was used to make free phone calls by capturing control of freephone (*0800*) trunks and re-routing them. Legend has it that the first of these tone generators was built into a small handheld blue box which is where the name came from.

The procedure, though initially difficult to work out, was in practice rather simple:

- First the Scammer would phone an *0800* number. *Before* the call was connected, the phreak tone would be sent. The trunk line would now be under the control of the Scammer.
- Next a tone known as the start-keying tone would be sent. Followed by the actual phone number to be contacted for free.
- Finally the end-keying tone would be sent and the call connected.

This procedure exploited a flaw inherent in all trunk lines. When the line was available for use it 'whistled' the *phreak* tone. *Routers* at the exchange would listen out for the tone that would indicate the availability of that line.

The UK Phreak Tones

0 →	1740 and 1860 Hz
1 →	1380 and 1500 Hz
2 →	1380 and 1620 Hz
3 →	1500 and 1620 Hz
4 →	1380 and 1740 Hz
5 →	1500 and 1740 Hz
6 →	1620 and 1740 Hz
7 →	1380 and 1860 Hz
8 →	1500 and 1860 Hz
9 →	1620 and 1860 Hz

Master Tone - 2280Hz

When the router found an available trunk line, the tone would be switched off and a call routed through it to the exchange at the far end. When the call was later disconnected the 'available for use' tone would come back on.

What the *Fone Phreak* was doing was connecting to the trunk and then sending down (just for a few seconds) the 'available for use' tone. This made the line think it was not in use when it was. The phone at the other end of the line would not ring, as the line did not realise that it was in use. Once inside the trunk, the Scammer could then reprogram it with their *blue box* and the call would be charged at the rate of whichever type of trunk it was. If it was an *0800* trunk the Scammer got free phone calls to anywhere else on the planet.

What did the *Fone Phreaks* do with this power? They talked. Oh, how they talked! The ones who talked the most were the blind kids. This was a medium where they came into their own. Cyberspace can be very accommodating to disadvantaged groups such as the physically incapacitated or the chronically shy.

To this day, legends still persist about the *USA's* famous *phreak*, the blind kid *Joe Engressia* (*Whistler*) who had perfect pitch and could whistle all of the phreaking tones. He was a living, breathing *blue box*.

A popular pastime for *phreaks* abroad was the collection of public callbox numbers that they would take back home and distribute amongst the phreak community. Have you ever been in a shopping mall and noticed a public phone ringing? It was possibly a *phreak* on the other end (maybe from another country) looking for a long chat.

Can you imagine the thrill of linking trunk line upon trunk line together through tens of thousands of miles of cables and switching circuits only to make the payphone beside you ring? No, either can I, but a phreak can!

Once computer hackers heard about blue boxing, it didn't take them long to discover that some modems could be used to send out *phreaking* tones. Failing that, the sound card of their computer systems could be programmed to produce those tones. To the hacker this was a dream come true.

The War Dialler

There was/is a software device about known as the *War Dialler.* Named after the device seen in operation in the successful motion picture *War Games*, the *War Dialler* was a program that automated the calling of a list of phone numbers. The Scammer would give it a start phone number and an end phone number. The *War Dialler* would then automatically call every number in-between those two numbers, listening for a pre-determined time for a *carrier* tone that would indicate the presence of a computer system on the other end of the line. If a *carrier* was discovered the phone number would be recorded in a list that the Scammer could later examine with a view to compromising that system.

Before *blue boxing* techniques, *War Diallers* were seldom used, as the cost of perhaps hundreds of phone calls would be too high for the average hacker. But *Blue boxing* made *War Dialling* an affordable sport.

More Boxes

Another very common trick of the *Fone Phreak* was the building and use of a *black box.* Why it was known as a *black box* is unknown (nearly all Fone Phreak equipment is known by colours and as a box) as the circuit was not in a box at all, but built into a telephone.

Basically a resistor was put in series with one of the telephone's incoming wires. A switch would also be added so that the modification could be switched on and off.

With a little ingenuity and a micro switch or relay, the telephone could be set up so that the black box circuit would cut in automatically when the phone was answered. A switch would still be needed to turn the circuit off should an out-going call be required.

The black-boxed phone would ring and be answered by the Scammer. Quickly the switch would be thrown to toggle the extra circuit into action. This restricted the voltage levels on the line to such a low level that the meter which was responsible for recording the calls cost would not work properly. So, the person who had made the call was *not* being charged.

Here are some other *phreak* boxes that were once very popular. Some of them still work and some of them never worked to start with.

Aqua Box

There is a legendary event that all *phreakers* dread. It is spoke of in hushed tones. It's the fabled *Lock In Trace* as supposedly used by the *FBI* and other such agencies. This is where a special mechanism is used to force the line to stay open so that the call can be traced. The *Aqua Box* was suppose to stop the *Lock In Trace* and allow the line to be disconnected. Don't believe a word of it; it would really muck up cop movies if there was such a thing as a *Lock In Trace.*

Assassin Box

This device was *supposed* to be used to give the person on the other end of the phone an electrical shock. Obviously it wouldn't work with modern phones, as there's very little metal on them, just plastic. Whether it worked in the good old days, I don't know. None of the *phreaks* I have known have ever tried it, but rumours abound.

Beige Box

This is just a normal telephone (the smaller the better) with the cable connector cut off and replaced with alligator clips. It could be used to patch into other peoples lines. There are junction boxes in most streets and on the ground floor of flats. These are ideal places to Beige box.

A friend of mine once heard two 'secret' homosexuals arranging to meet up for sex whilst one's spouse was in hospital and the other's was out of the country. Luckily for them, he wasn't into blackmail.

Blast Box

It is not a good idea to upset a *Fone Phreak.* You may find that your home phone number is re-routed to a sex line. But if you really bother them, they may hook up an amplifier to the phone and dial your number. When you answer, the amplifier will switch on and you'll be deafened or at least have trouble hearing anything for several hours. This is the *Blast Box.*

Blotto Box

Named after a *phreak* called *King Blotto,* this is a legendary device that is supposed to destroy whole telephone Networks. Now, while it is possible to remotely damage lines and junction boxes, it is unlikely that a whole Network could be brought down. After all, telephone systems can withstand *1.21* gigawatts of electricity generated in a lightning strike (see *Back To The Future* for further details). And, if it were that easy, one of the more socially-irresponsible *phreaks* would have already done it.

Red Box

When a coin is put into a pay phone it sends a tone to the exchange. The red box simulates these tones so the exchange thinks that coins have been deposited and therefore the call is *effectively* free. An alternative is to record the tones as coins drop into the coin slot. At a later date, the recording can be played back down the handset, thus giving free calls.

Charging Box

The *Charging Box* is used to indicate when a call is being charged for and when it is not. The box has two *LED's* on it. One shows that the phreak has successfully made a free call. The other shows that the call is being charged in the normal way.

Clear Box

This was a simple device, which only worked on old style phone boxes. Those phones didn't require payment until *after* the connection was established and the caller could not be heard *until* after payment was deposited.

The Clear Box was a small amplifier and a telephone pick-up induction coil (one of those things with the suckers). The pick-up coil would be plugged into the *output* of the amplifier and a microphone plugged into the *input.*

In use, the Scammer would speak through the microphone instead of the handset. Their voice went through the amplifier, out of the induction coil into the phone system. The party at the other end could now hear the caller.

Box-mania

Plans are readily available on the Internet for an awful lot of different phreaking related devices such as mauve, brown, silver, yellow, white, scarlet, crimson and other boxes. For some bizarre reason, rather a lot of these tutorials and plans do not actually mention what the device does. The writers assume that the reader already knows what a purple with green spots and white stripes box does.

Pearl Box

Basically, a programmable version of the *blue box*, which meant that it could be used in any country regardless of what the local *phreaking* tones were.

Phreaking Today

What about today's *Fone Phreaks*? This method of cyber exploitation is becoming rarer and will shortly die out all together. In the *UK* the modern digital exchange is equipped with filters to take out extraneous *2280* Hertz tones. The *phreaking* tone has to be *very* loud to get through at all. If it is *too* loud an alarm will ring in the exchange and the call will be traced in seconds. Effectively, this means that *blue boxing* is really only practical on older analogue exchanges or remote public call boxes.

There are still ways in which to exploit the phone companies, but they are mostly in the hands of the telephone company's *own* engineers who ain't above doing a bit of rewiring to suit themselves or a paying customer. I have known such engineers. Not a lot of people realise that the *Jim Carey* film, *The Cable Guy*, was *actually* a documentary.

The text below contains the highlights of a rather long and extremely interesting conversation with *Jack Wraith of the* ***Telecommunications UK Fraud Forum (www.tuff.co.uk).***

"[One] real problem regarding phone fraud and abuse [down to] professionally organised crime gangs. Their targets are the telephone exchanges of large authorities and business.

They often hit the private telephone exchanges of companies, hospitals and schools for vast remunerations. Typically, they will get someone to hack into the exchange (which in today's Internet world is often easier than you would think) and get them to seditiously patch their own lines into the circuits.

They will then hire premises in a high visibility place like the high street and equip it with these acquired effectively free (or low cost) telephone lines. Ethnic communities will be targeted regarding cut-price phone calls to their home countries.

With such services offered at a considerable fraction of their true cost, the customer base for these fraudsters is more or less assured. The fraudster knows that the chances of being caught are considerably lessened if such activity takes place during the hours the company is closed for the weekend or, as in the case of educational establishments, closed for the summer months.

The maximum punishment for this sort of crime as specified by the Telecom's Act can be up to five years in jail. In practice, no one is likely to serve more than 2 to 3 years. Examples of such fraud are not hard to come by. One such is what happened to a UK organisation that was defrauded of resources over an 18-month period before the illegal activity came to light. They lost approximately £750,000. The company's name was the Metropolitan Police.

Telephone fraudsters do not have it all their own way. Telecommunication Companies are becoming much more sophisticated in using technology to detect and catch such people.

Automated alarms can be installed on lines that will be triggered on just about any event that they are told to. For example, the trigger could be that if a private company' s exchange has calls over the weekend the alarm is activated.

Another trigger may be the amount of calls (or the cost of calls) over a predetermined period.

With all this (and much more) going on, is it any wonder that British Telecom Operators are increasingly putting more resources and manpower into this area of crime? A number of these companies now have whole departments dedicated to detecting and preventing telephone fraud."

When the going gets *TUFF*, the *TUFF* get going?

Chapter Seven

Info Junkies

"...I do not possess the kind of information necessary; I do not possess the kind of intelligence; I want guiding. There is no man in this world on whom I could so rely for right guidance..."
- A Tale of Two Cities, Charles Dickens

The original *Information Junkies* are the librarian, the writer and the researcher. They reached cyberspace before anyone else. They need their information like a dog needs a bone... Like an alcoholic needs a drink... Like a fish needs water... Like a woman needs chocolate... They simply *love* information - the more bizarre and the dodgier the better.

Cyberspace is a heaven to the *Information Junkie*. Texts and tutorials can be easily found on matters as diverse as *Cracking, Hacking, Murdering, Disposing Of Bodies, Phreaking, Bomb Making, Lock Picking, Carding, Chipping, House Breaking, Blackmail, Security, Pirating, Anarchy* and *Terrorism.*

Although digging up information is easy, the difficult part is recognising the real stuff from the rubbish (of which there is a lot). You'll find texts on bomb making that were written by a kid taking first-grade chemistry, and plenty of other stuff by writers who seldom test out their ideas before releasing them into cyberspace. That flamethrower may look fun to build but would be more likely to blow you up than throw flames.

Other texts are just plain lies; like the 'fact' that you can get unmetered phone calls on your mobile if you remove and boil the *SIMM* for half an hour, or the idea that you can get high by smoking peanut skins.

The bizarre thing is, a surprisingly large quantity of people will fall for things like this and try them. The true *Information Junkie* rarely tries out what they discover. They climb the mountain because it's there.

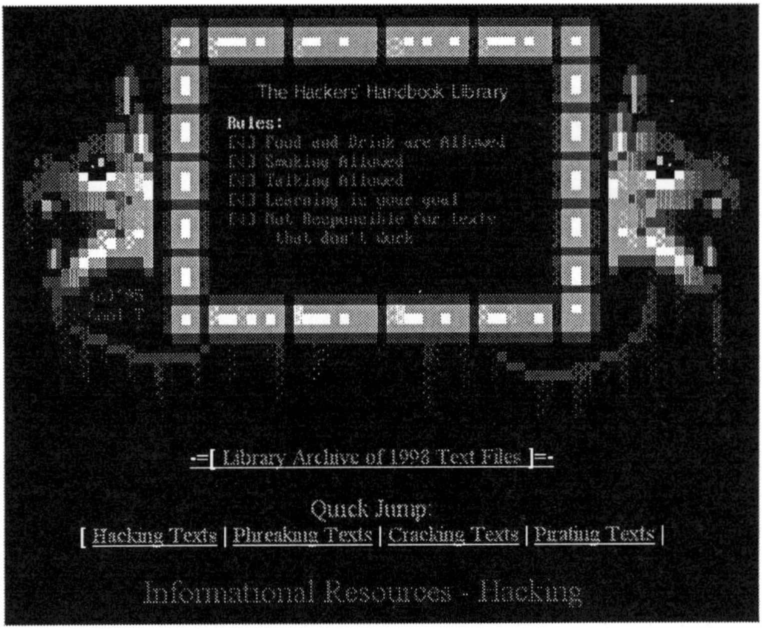

Some *Information Junkies* collect software as well as information. Indeed, some of the biggest collections of cracked software in the world are in the hands of people who will never even use the programs let alone profit by them - but then that *is* the nature of collectors.

The fun is in assembling the collection *not* in doing anything with it. With *Information Junkies* in particular, there is a thrill in knowing that you know something that others don't. It's fun to know you *could* do these things, but choose *not* to do so.

Websites containing forbidden knowledge attract data junkies like flies to a dung heap. The countries which exercise an excessive amount of freedom of speech have a lot to answer for. The US first amendment gives the citizen the right to the resource of forbidden knowledge. And since US websites are accessible from anywhere on the planet...

God bless America!

Not that this information is always of a particularly interesting nature. There are websites dedicated to pylons, holes, pumps and other such mind staggeringly interesting things.

Here's a classic example. One of my favourites is an archive dedicated to very old pirated software. A shrine to the cracking groups from the dark ages. Legends such as *The Medway Boys, Pompey Pirates, Sewer Disks*, and *Automation*. Every compilation disk they ever made listed and available for download. To anyone who lived through those times, they were magical indeed. Games that, if bought though retailers, would take up maybe as many as three - five uncopyable disks. These were routinely unprotected, highly compressed in a still-executable format and dumped on a floppy with a fancy menu with graphics and sound.

The juicy stuff to the collectors were the 'scrollies'. These were long text messages which would scroll from one side of the screen to the other. These would contain *"greets"* (greetings) and insults from the hackers and crackers to other groups. Very often there would be details on how the games had been cracked or the adventures of the group's individuals.

Normal computer users would buy one of these disks from their local pirate only if they had a game on them that they could not afford through normal means. But to the information junkies they were collected for the sake of it. Each scrolly savoured and discussed in great depth.

Why? What is the point? And that is where it all fizzles out. There are no answers. Something's just *are*. The mountain is climbed because it is there.

Information junkies - know things. Secret things. Real things.

Spot the Hoax

"Dear Internet Subscriber: Please read the following carefully if you intend to stay online and continue using email: The last few months have revealed an alarming trend in the Government of the United States attempting to quietly push through legislation that will affect your use of the Internet.

Under proposed legislation (Bill 602P) the U.S. Postal service will be attempting to bulk email users out of "alternative postage fees". Bill 602P will permit the Federal Govt. to charge 5 cents surcharge on every email delivered, by billing Internet Service Providers at source. The consumer would then be billed in turn by the ISP.

Washington D.C. lawyer Richard Stepp is working without pay to prevent this legislation from becoming law. The U.S. Postal Service is claiming that lost revenue due to the proliferation of email is costing nearly $230,000,000 in revenue per year. You may have noticed the recent ad campaign "There is nothing like a letter".

Since the average citizen received about 10 pieces of email per day in 1998, the cost to the typical individual would be an additional 50 cents per day, or over $180 per year, above and beyond their regular Internet costs. Note that this would be money paid directly to the U.S. Postal Service for a service they do not even provide. The whole point of the Internet is democracy and non-interference.

If the Federal Govt. is permitted to tamper with our liberties by adding a surcharge to email, who knows where it will end. You are already paying an exorbitant price for snail mail because of bureaucratic inefficiency."

Email of unknown origin

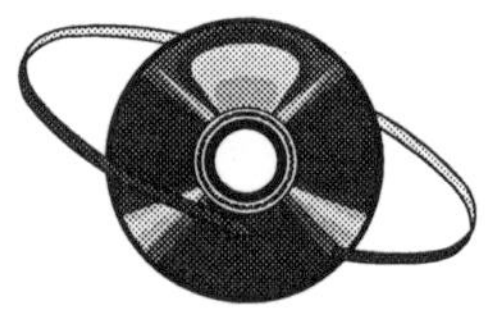

Chapter Eight

Newsgroup Scams

"...Mainhall was a good gossip who always knew what had been going on in town; especially, he knew everything that was not printed in the newspapers..."
- Alexander's Bridge, Willa Cather

Newsgroups are great resources for the cyber Scammer. They can gain knowledge of everything from learning to pickpocket to building their own atomic bomb (I kid you not).

Here are some examples of the sort of diversity of Newsgroups that are available. To keep things interesting, one of the following Newsgroups is a fake. Can you guess which one?

a.bsu.religion
a.bsu.talk
a.business.internet
a2i.ba.jobs.offered
alt.arts.origami
alt.binaries.pics.asparagus
alt.binaries.pictures.babies
alt.binaries.x-files
alt.chips.salt-n-vinegar
alt.collecting.bicycles
alt.comedy.british
alt.conspiracy
alt.culture.luddites
alt.doityourself.proctology
alt.drinks.beer
alt.drugs.caffeine
alt.drunken.bastards
alt.drwho.creative
alt.Esperanto
alt.fan.adolf-hitler
alt.homosexuality
alt.infertility
alt.life.universe.everything
alt.penpals.50-plus
alt.politics.socialism
alt.startrek.books
alt.startrek.cardassian
alt.support.dental-phobia
alt.support.depression
alt.support.diabetes
alt.support.domestic-vio
alt.support.jock-strap
alt.teens.penpals
alt.toys.marbles.bc
alt.toys.my-little-pony
alt.tv.a-team

alt.tv.avengers
alt.tv.babylon5
biz.healthcare
bremnet.secondhand
can.community.asian
christnet.philosophy
dc.graphics.avs
dc.ham-radio
dc.media
dc.music
dc.org.linux-users
dc.politics
dc.redskins
dc.romance
misc.rural
misc.survivalism
misc.taxes
talk.atheism
talk.bizarre
talk.environment
talk.euthanasia

The act of placing a message in a newsgroup is known as posting. Newsgroups can be public (posting and reading is allowed) or private (only reading is allowed).

There are two sub categories of public Newsgroups. One is the *discussion* group. The other is a *binary* group. In the former only information in the form of *American Standard Code for Information Interchange* (*ASCII*) permitted. This is a plain vanilla flavoured form of text. In the latter, data and program files can be attached to the message and also sent. A popular pastime amongst the *binaries* is the exchange of cracks, patches, freeware, shareware, bug fixes, pictures (*gif* and *jpeg* format) and music files (*MP3*).

One particularly unsavoury scam in some Newsgroups is the swapping of books currently still in copyright. No doubt that this work will end up in them. Using *Optical Character Recognition* (*OCR*) software, the volume is scanned in and converted to a text or Portable Document Format (*PDF*). Typical targets for this type of exploitation are the works of *Terry Pratchett*, *Stephen King* or any best selling author.

With temptations like this (imagine reading the latest blockbuster months before it is officially released) is it any wonder that **alt.binaries.e-book** is one of the most popular Newsgroups of all time.

alt.doityourself.proctology is the false newsgroup

And that's not all. Anything, which can be stored digitally, is regularly scammed. All the latest *USA* video releases are obtainable for download months before they are even released in the *UK*.

The Touch of the Trolls

Generally the people who frequent Newsgroups are decent enough sorts, but there *are* extremists in cyberspace and they often hang out in Newsgroups. There are fascist groups, racist groups, terrorist groups and many other groups that the average person would be uncomfortable with. Don't be completely put off, however, as for every racist, bigot, chauvinist or person of an extreme or anti-social viewpoint there are hundreds of decent educated people exchanging their views in a proper manner. The Newsgroups are the Internets ultimate *right of reply.*

But - on the other hand - if a cyber Scammer wants someone to stalk, Newsgroups (or chat rooms) are a good place to start. Some of the more unsavoury frequenters of Newsgroups are known as *trolls.* Indeed, if you ever go anywhere near a Newsgroup you will eventually bump into one. A *troll* is a person who flits from newsgroup to newsgroup spreading paranoia, distrust, arguments and generally causing trouble.

They do this for fun. Some of them can be quite tame, but others would make the crudest of comedians blush. They don't last too long in chat rooms as the moderators purge them or several other users keep *pinging* the culprits until their connection fails. But in the Newsgroups the *trolls* really come into their own.

An Example - The ISA Troll

One summer one of the lesser known hacking and warez Newsgroups of *UseNet* was targeted by a particularly nasty *troll* with the handle *I Said Ass (ISA).* Their nickname was not actually this, it was something infinitely fouler.

This attack was made possible due to the use of an *anonymous remailer.* This is a software device that allows emails to be sent through a special server that strips off identification codes and re-sends the email onto its final destination.

While such a thing has legitimate uses, the remailer is often abused and is the *trolls'* best friend. Remailing servers do not usually last long and end up being shut down due to excessive complaints. Technically, a court order can be issued that forces the owner of the server to give access to their records, but I have yet to hear of anyone being prosecuted for malicious anonymous emailing or newsgroup posting. However, I digress...

Due to the nature of the postings that took place during the incident and I am *not* going to quote directly from them, but just give you the gist of what went on. Where I have left a profanity in, you can be assured that the original was *much* worse. It all started with something like this.

"Hi guys. I've got some really great kiddie porn for sale at really competitive prices. You just will not believe some of the things my nine-year-old gets up to! Little Carol is some hot bitch! Email me for details. Anonymity guaranteed. All videos posted under a plain wrapper. Money back if not satisfied."

I Said Ass

Like any decent human beings, the hackers and pirates responded with a tirade of abuse and told *ISA* where to go and where they would stick their videos if they caught him. *ISA* ignored this and continued to re-post the same notice and similar under different topic headings.

After a while the hackers and pirates stopped responding to ISA and began to ignore him instead. *ISA* stopped posting the notices. After a few weeks everyone had forgotten about him. Then...

"Hi morons! Remember me? I have been compiling a list of you lamers now for months and you are all dead. I've been buying your so called crappy warez for some time now just so that I could get your addresses and I've just given them all to FAST. You scum suckers are ali going to shortly get knocks on your doors at three in the morning from the pigs. Remember when CAPTAIN FORMAT got busted last month? That was me wot grassed him up. Got well paid for it. You are all in my book. I'm going to be very well off and when your asses are all in jail, I'm going to start selling your warez at £2 a disk. You just cannot compete with me!

I am king ass! I Said (I Said Ass) Ass. I am one muther of a scumsucker. I will see you squirm! I will see you die! Screw you all and the horse you rode in on!!!! Hahahaha!"

I Said Ass

And do you know something? I think he was right. He was indeed an *ass*. The hackers and pirates just told him to *eff* off and otherwise ignored him. *ISA* posted dozens of notices all along the same lines stating the same thing with constantly varying profanity and all manner of different threats. Eventually, tempers got frayed and people started to reply to his rantings. And then...

"Hello people. I ordered some disks off of that I Said Ass group and they are great! High quality, quick delivery and only £2 each. Why don't you give it a go? The worst thing that can happen is you lose two pounds."

Stag Beatle

Quite a few notices (seemingly from different people) like that one appeared in the newsgroup. When the hackers examined the headers on the postings, they had all originated from the same anonymous remailer server that *ISA's* messages came from. *ISA* wasn't fooling anyone.

Then the forgery started. Messages were posted that appeared to be from the Newsgroups regulars, but which also had the same anonymous remailer header.

"Hey guys! Have you heard the latest? Electric TomCat got busted last night! They battered his door down in the middle of the night and took just about everything in his house and gave him an intrusive search (no I don't know why either). They gave him a good kicking too!"

Adam Ant

"Yes, I was there too at Electric TomCat's house when it happened. They gave him some kicking! I was lucky that I managed to get away when I did without them spotting me to!"

Petal

"I found this news interesting as I don't remember it happening and wasn't even at home last night?"
Electric TomCat

Several people complained to the owners of the anonymous remailer server in question that *ISA* had been using, but nothing was done about it. *ISA* started to issue more threats. And then.

"Dear, I Said Ass. Stop this behaviour immediately or face the consequences. I know who you are and you know who I am and we both know I am NOT to be messed with. One more of these posts and I'll be visiting you in the middle of the night with a few friends."
Vim

This message and other similar ones also came from the same anonymous remailer Server. *I Said Ass* was threatening to beat himself up! The regulars tried to reason with *ISA*, but this did not work. Eventually everyone started to get annoyed by all this.

"Look guys! I Said Ass is just a troll. He wants to provoke a reaction in us. That's how he gets his kicks. Don't answer anything he says. Ignore him and he will go away. Better still, put him in your newsreaders killfile and you'll never see him again."
Electric TomCat

This was good advice. The trouble was that (although they would not admit it) every body was dying to see what would happen next. More forgeries followed as well as more threats and lies.

ISA posted details of several people's home addresses, telephone numbers and claimed to have sent their details to hundreds of pornographic and other undesirable organisations.

Again, this did not fool anyone. For a start, the people whose addresses were purported to have been posted denied it and the dialling codes of the telephone numbers did not match those of the addresses. Nevertheless, doubt, suspicion and chaos began to run rampant within the newsgroup.

Everyone had their own views on how to deal with *ISA* and they started to argue amongst themselves. *ISA* loved this! Eventually, the regulars split into two factions. Those who had decided to use encryption methods to sign and/or encrypt their postings and those who thought that this was a bad idea. This caused *more* arguing.

After a while of increasingly nasty abuse from *ISA* the regulars had had enough. They decided to track him down and take the law into their own hands. A plan of action was discussed using private email messages. Before it could be implemented, *ISA* vanished.

The last word in this matter was this posting sent a few days later from the same anonymous remailer server.

"Hello peeps! This is a really nice newsgroup you all have here."
Secret Squirrel

For the time being, the attack was over. During the course of events, it was interesting to note that everybody assumed that the attacker was male. Why this was so, I don't know as nothing was found out about them at all. Not their sex, age, location or anything else. Even hackers can become the victims of the cyber Scammer.

In the long run, this *troll* attack appears to have done something that the *Federation Against Software Theft* (*FAST*) could not do.

Having seen or been told of the havoc that ISA had caused, other trolls stuck their noses into the newsgroup. The end result was that several of the warez pirates stopped trading. Not because they were scared of events, but because they were sick to death of the whole carry on. In the end, no one could trust anyone anymore.

More than one person has since speculated that these *trolls* were actually organised by *FAST* or a similar organisation. Whilst this is an interesting idea, it is unrealistic, but then again, you never know who is out there doing what or why.

In cyberspace as in real life, sometimes, things just ain't the way they seem...

Protect Yourself

What can you do to protect yourself in a newsgroup? For a start there are two types of newsgroup. *UseNet* is where the real sicko's hang out (but it's mostly nice people).

My *Internet Server Provider's* (*ISP*) news server has over 50,000 different *UseNet* groups on it and has a mail flow approaching a million items per day!

A nicer alternative to *UseNet* is to use *forums* (or *fora*), which are local to a particular server or provider. A *forum* is just another name for a newsgroup. *Forums* are more restricted and better moderated than *UseNet* and contain much fewer groups. You can still get the same problems in *forums* as on *UseNet* but on a smaller scale and the *forum trolls* aren't quite so nasty because they can be easily caught and banned by their *ISP*.

One of the first things you should do on installing your newsreader software is to install a *Spam Trap*. Take a look at this message header?

From: Sting <sting@NOSPAMpublichouse.com>
To: Newsgroups: alt.internet.coding
Subject: my website
Date: Mon, 10 Jul 2002 17:18:26 +0100
Message-ID: <eitjmskpt2p6l1pufr8tsjov79p8s6bn15@4ax.com>
X-Newsreader: Forte Agent 1.8

Notice the words *NOSPAM* in the middle of the sender's email address? This addition is known as a *Spam Trap*.

So what is *Spam*, do I hear you ask and why would you want to trap it? Well *Spam* is a type of cold meat popular in sandwiches or in salads. It is also cyber talk for unsolicited email or advertisements in Newsgroups (which most *ISPs* do not allow anyway, but *Spammers* still do it). It can be very annoying to download from your favourite newsgroup only to discover hundred of copies of the same advert (usually for a product that is pretty lame and wouldn't sell anyway).

The *Spammer* will also trawl the Newsgroups looking for email addresses so that they can send their advert straight to their victim's inbox. What they do is to send out a *spider* or *bot* (both are web robots) into the Newsgroups to search through literally millions of messages for the @ sign. If it finds one, it assumes that it has just discovered someone's email address and adds it to a list, which it eventually sends back to the *Spammers*. This list can contain several *million* addresses and, as such, is too big to be checked.

This is where the *Spam Trap* comes into play. Any extra text added into an email address will invalidate that email address. When the *Spammers* mail shot is executed, the *Spam Trapped* address cannot be used.

To a normal sender, the *Spam Trap* can be seen and removed so that that they are able to send a message to a valid address. With millions of people using *Spam Traps*, it is impossible for the *Spammer* to remove all the traps.

They could instruct the bot to look for the words *NOSPAM* within an address and remove it, but this would be pointless as a *Spam Trap* can be any text at all. Here are some popular examples.

datajunkieNOSPAM@bigfoot.com
datajunkieNO@SPAMbigfoot.com
datajunkie@REMOVETHISbigfoot.com
datajunkieSPAMMERS@SUCKbigfoot.com
datajunkieYOU_KNOW@WHAT_TO_Dobigfoot.com
datajunkieNO@THANKSbigfoot.com
datajunkie @ bigfoot.com

Traditional responses to *Spam* range from ignoring the sender to *mail-bombing* them. A *mail-bomb* is a piece of software designed by hackers/crackers that sends several copies (hundreds of thousands if necessary) of an abusive email (or one full of rubbish) back to the originator of the *Spam,* thus giving the *Spammer* a taste of their own medicine.

Mailbombing software can be found on just about every shareware and freeware website for *"...educational purposes only..."*.

Address Harvesting

The collection (also known as *"data mining"*) of email addresses from Newsgroups or websites, with the intention of spamming those addresses (or selling to other spammers with less technical knowledge) is known as 'harvesting'. Software ro(bots) cruise the Internet looking for email addresses entirely on their own. Once found, the address is sent back to a central database where it is added or discarded through filters. Sometimes the spam traps are spotted and removed. Other times useless addresses are added to the database. If computer viruses can be thought of as the lowest form of artificial life, then the web bot could be considered the next stage up.

Of course, if bots can harvest email addresses, they can data-mine for other information. As full blown automated resources, the bot's potential as a hacking tool is considerable. They are capable of searching out specific forms of information and then performing actions on this data depending on the results of, sometimes quite complex groups, of logical operations. Indexing, collating, redistributing and (if the user permissions have not been set correctly or can be changed) even deleting, creating or adjusting information.

Pornography

"He had no further intercourse with Spirits, but lived upon the Total Abstinence Principle..." - A Christmas Carol, Charles Dickens

Tabloid newspapers love to report about pornography in cyberspace. It's everywhere! It's sick! It's degrading! Kids can easily get it! I'd like to say that it isn't at all true, but I can't. It *is* everywhere and kids *can* get it easily.

Pornography is a multi-billion-dollar/pound industry in cyberspace. In fact, the pornography industry has much more power than the average person is aware of. For example did you know that it was due to pornography that *VHS* got chosen over *Betamax* as the home video tape standard simply because there was so much pornography available in that format?

Don't think that just because *you* are uninterested in such things that they can be ignored. If you use *any* Newsgroups at all, you will have to download the list of *all* available Newsgroups. You might not be using them, but the details are still on your hard disk for any curious kid, or investigating officer, to find.

Be warned!! A particularly prevalent '*joke*' in Newsgroups is to post a reply to a commonly asked beginner's question. The reply will contain a link to somewhere nasty. For example, here is a posting from the British hacker group **alt.ph.uk**

"Does anyone know how to hack a Vodafone so that I can get free phone calls?"

To which came the reply...

"Sorry, but I do not know anything about this kind of thing. Click on the link below to be taken to a website that can probably help."

At the time, I was researching phones (I didn't post the original message - honest!) and was curious so I clicked on the link. The page that appeared in the browser contained a disclaimer and a picture of a man holding his prolapsed anus open extremely wide.

"Disclaimer : If you find this picture offensive then please do not look at it."

Whilst I am not easy to shock, this picture would have been extremely upsetting to most people. Remember that Newsgroups are a public place and are often frequented by the very young. Would you like this happening to your ten year old?

You'll find some specific do's and don'ts relating to Internet porn in Chapter 11.

From and Reply-to

The FROM address is the email address that you see as the recipient of an email. However, the REPLY-TO address is the actual return email address. If there is no REPLY-TO address specified then the FROM is used by default.
If someone wanted to send you an email of the spam variety, and suspected that you were running a filter which would dump it into the trash folder, they could put a fake address in the FROM field and the real one in the REPLY-TO field. The filter would not catch the spam and you would not realise who had actually sent it until you click on 'reply' and the real email address appears in the header of the reply that you were about to write.

Chapter Nine

Virus Vandalism

"Man has been endowed with reason, with the power to create, so that he can add to what he's been given. But up to now he hasn't been a creator, only a destroyer..."
- Uncle Vanya, Anton Checkhov

Computer nasties have been about since Babbage's Day. Does anyone remember going into a their local computer store in the 80's? Typing something like the following program into one of the display machines and then running away?

```
10 PRINT "This store is a load of rubbish!!!"
20 GOTO 10
```

Later, when *PCs* came out, you went back to the store to persecute them further by doctoring the *AUTOEXEC.BAT* files in every display machine to something like this.

```
echo You have just been hacked by Flash Gordon!
Hahahaha!
pause
```

To make things better, the staff of those early computer stores rarely knew how to fix the problem.

Well, actually, I never did anything like that either, but if you know someone who did (and the interest in computers stayed with them) then there is a very real chance that they went onto write a computer virus.

Why do people write viruses? Ask any form of vandal that question and they will probably shrug disinterestedly and say,

"D'know?" If they're particularly bright they might add, *"Cause I can!"* And that is why virus writers write viruses. Because they can.

What exactly is a computer virus?

It is the name given to a piece of computer code that can primarily duplicate itself and secondarily (though not always implemented) have a detrimental effect to the well being of the infected computer system.

They can range from the classic harmless but annoying *Cookie* virus (which just keeps on asking the user to type in the word "cookie" at random times), to real nasties like the infamous *ILoveYou* Visual Basic Script (*VBS)* email virus which deletes files and sends copies of itself to every body in your address book.

Viruses don't necessarily strike immediately. By the time it is triggered (by a date/time or event), it may have been on your computer for weeks and, as such, managed to spread itself all over the place.

It is generally thought that viruses can only damage software and that hardware is safe. This is a common misconception. A virus can force the hard drive to continually recalibrate itself. If this happens when the user is away from the computer for a long time it will eventually damage the drive.

Also, more and more viruses are being designed that can

Private Viruses

Lots of virus writers create viruses that are never sent out into the *wild*. Instead, they send them off to anti-virus companies to show off what they can do.

Some of them correspond with such companies regularly and some are even *rumoured* to get paid for this work. They supposedly get very well paid if they come up with a new technique *before* it is detected in the wild. Some of these techniques were invented years ago and cures already exist for yet-to-be created viruses.

wipe the *CMOS* of its host computer. The *CMOS* is the tiny segment of computer code that allows the computer to start up (to boot).

Luckily, all you need to do to fix this type of attack is to open the computer's case and remove the *CMOS* back-up battery for a while or (if it has one) 'short' the *CMOS* jumper. But while your average hardware junkie would know this fact, the more normal user might end up having to call an expensive computer repairman.

Another vulnerable part of the computer is the *BIOS* (Basic Input Output System). This is more commonly stored on an *Electrically Erasable Programmable Read Only Memory* (EEPROM). This is where the boot code for the computer is stored and if it gets wiped (Flashed) the computer becomes junk. Luckily this is pretty hard to do for a virus coder, but they could target specific motherboards if they took the time to examine the BIOS firmware.

Common Virus Nomenclature

Boot Sector Virus

A virus that infects only the boot sector on a floppy disk. These viruses are particularly serious because information already present in the boot sector, such as the operating system loader, will be over written.

Companion Virus

This uses a similar name and the rules of program precedence to associate itself with a regular program. This kind of virus is also referred to as a *spawning* virus.

Dropper

An executable file that, when run, "*drops*" a virus. When this kind of file is scanned, the scan will not detect a virus, because the actual virus code is not created until the *Parent* file has been executed.

Executable Infector

This attaches itself to, or associates itself with, a file. This type of virus usually attaches to the beginning or end of regular program files.

Hoax
This is usually an email that warns of a non-existent or a valid virus that does more harm in spreading fear than an actual virus. Joke programs also exist which makes the user think that their system is being attacked when it is in fact just a harmless fake error message. A typical program may run a simulation of the hard drive being formatted.

Macro Virus
A *Macro Virus* is a deliberately coded, malicious, auto-run macro most commonly associated with word processors and spreadsheets. The macro may be designed to cause damage to the system and/or replicate itself.

The *Macro* virus exploits a type of computer scripting language that was originally designed to automate the tedious task of complex word processing tasks. These viruses infect documents and can have similar effects to the more traditional type of virus. They cannot be run outside of the macros environment.

MBR Virus
This is exactly the same as a boot sector virus except that it attacks the *Master Boot Record* on the hard drive's main partition.

Polymorphic Virus
A virus that attempts to evade detection by changing its own structure by using encryption techniques.

Stealth Virus
This uses various sneaky techniques to avoid detection, see below.

Worm
Technically this is not a virus as it usually spreads via email or *Internet Relay Chat,* but it is just as harmful as any virus. Usually created using some sort of scripting language.

As you can see from the above, there are several types of virus. The most common virus is the *executable* infector. This adds its own header code to the beginning of a program file, which does its evil deed before running the actual program.

The upshot of this is that an infected file gets slightly bigger. This used to be a good indicator that a virus was present until someone invented *stealth* code. The *stealth* virus takes note of the size of the file *before* it infects it. After infection it will hack into the operating system and adjust the file size so that it the file still looks the same size as when it was uninfected (Well, it's not quite like that, but you get the fundamental idea). The only way to detect such a virus is to search for code segments within the infected program that matches a known virus key.

> ### *Virus Kits*
>
> There are virus development/creation kits available in cyberspace. This includes an infamous *WP Macro* viruses creation kit available for Microsoft Word.

The virus detection process can be further complicated by the introduction of the *Dark Avengers mutation engine* that let the virus modify its own code (*Polymorphic*) after a predetermined generation of copies.

These days, self-modifying and encrypted viruses are commonplace. At the moment there are in excess of 53,000 known viruses about. I have never had a virus on any of my *PCs* as I've always been very careful (not to mention lucky), but I have dealt with the *Evil Dropper Trojan*, the *Tequila* virus, the *Ghost* virus, the *Friday the 13th* virus and a couple of *WP Macro* viruses.

The Achilles Heal

The *Trojan* (named after the *Trojan* horse) is a program that looks like a nice game or utility, but actually contains some seditious code placed there by a hacker or cracker as a means to an end. Here are details of some popular Trojans.

3 Troj

This makes the printer spit out paper and also increases the paper's weight *10* fold by soaking it with ink. It can also freeze a computer. Luckily, it only works in *DOS*.

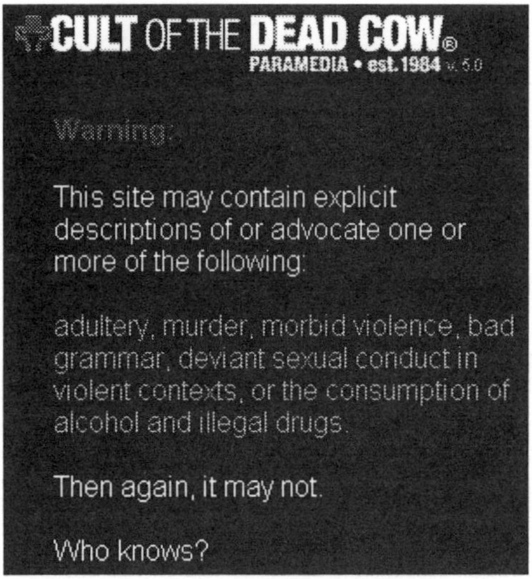

Back Orifice

This very popular Trojan by *The Cult Of The Dead Cow* installs a client/server on the target computer, which allows the Scammer full access to the computer's resources. It attempts to run as a hidden process allowing hackers to secretly use the target computer and listens on ports *TCP 31337, 54321* and *54320.* Now available for download on the Internet!

Big Brother

Nothing to do with the TV program of the same name. After several reboots, it will destroy the C drive of the target computer.

Buttons

This is designed to annoy the hell out of the user by opening hundreds of dialog boxes.

Cutev

Achieves the same by moving the mouse or opening Windows Notepad at random intervals.

Fire Killer

Removes all anti-virus and firewall products or just damages them to the extent that they need to be re-installed.

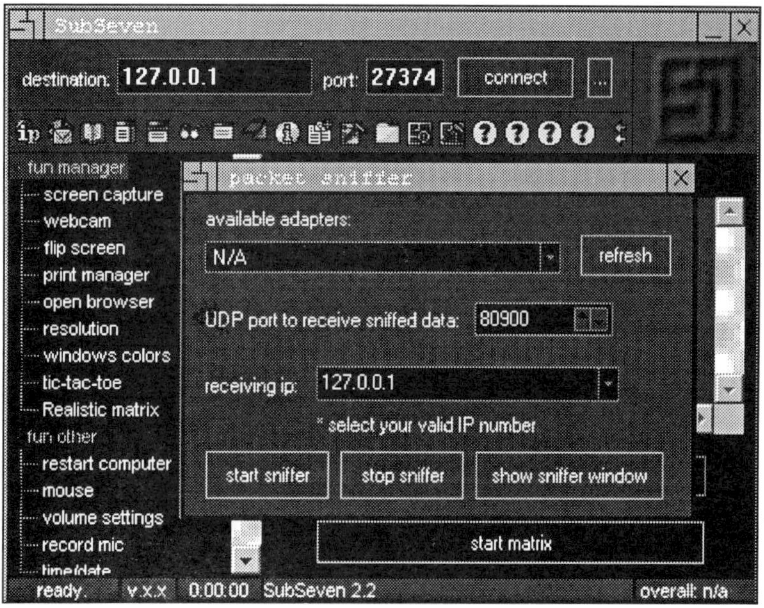

Hooker
Logs every single keystroke and mouse click made on the target computer.

NetBus
Quite an old (but sophisticated) *Trojan*. It can find cached passwords, has full control over all windows, can capture video from a video input device, has a scheduler to run scripts on specified hosts at a certain time, and support for plugins. It takes control of ports *12345*, *12456* and *20034 TCP*. Net*Bus Pro* is now available.

SubSeven
This is probably the most sophisticated *Trojan* ever created. It's like a super version of *Back Orifice* and Net*Bus* combined. It has its own address book, *WWW* page retriever, remote *IP* scanner, host lookup, *ICQ* takeover, retrieves dial-up passwords along with phone numbers and usernames, port redirector, make folders, delete folders, reboot server, instant messenger spy, file editor, mouse mover/clicker, set/change screen saver settings, can

reboot *Windows*, a very fast *IP* scanner and *IP* tool. On top of all that, it can often get the user's details from their *ISP* and other nice tricks. Now *that's* what I call Spyware!

Email Viruses

The latest type of virus is the email virus (often a *VB* Script), which usually exploits some security holes in *Microsoft's Internet Explorer* and/or *Outlook Express.*

Most users have become aware of these viruses and know that they should never run an unknown file that is attached to an email (especially if it is from someone they don't know) without scanning it first.

What is *not* readily known by most Internet users is that *any* executable file or script can be disguised as a picture or music file (or *any* data file) by a simple method that will fool the recipient into running it.

This is made possible by the fact that *Windows* can now use very long file names that include spaces and periods.

Have a look at this filename.

nicepicture.jpg   .exe

You see the problem? It is possible for the Scammer to put that many blank spaces within a filename that the end of the name (the *.exe* bit) is pushed off the edge of the screen.

All the recipient sees is the filename **nicepicture.jpg**. Thinks it's a picture file and double-clicks on it to open it (it does not work in *all* applications as some of them will show the whole file name wrapped). The malicious program is activated. If it is a *Trojan* like *Back Orifice* it can now do its job.

As if this was not bad enough, a *Trojan* could add a key to the *Windows* registry that tells it that a particular file extension - say BHJ - is to be treated as an executable file type and another key saying that any files with that extension must *not* show that extension.

```
HKEY_LOCAL_MACHINE\System\CurrentControlSet\Cont
rol\Session Manager\Environment\PATHEXT
.COM;.EXE;.BAT;.CMD;.VBS;.VBE;
.JS;.JSE;.WSF;.WSH;.BHJ

HKEY_CLASSES_ROOT\BHJ
"NeverShowExt"="0"
```

Therefore, a file called...

nicepicture.jpg.bhj

Would be displayed in *all* applications as...

nicepicture.jpg

And when the file was opened (...the birds began to sing...) the *Trojan* would be executed and be able to do its dirty deed. Consider a programmer of legitimate software who could easily put a piece of code in his company's product that would add those two keys during all installs.

Then if the programmer is later sacked, they could do a lot of damage to the company's reputation by sending out email attachments that include malicious code with the hidden executable extension.

If this is not bad enough, doing the rounds on the Internet is a prototype of an email virus that runs if the message is just looked at.

Damage for Art's Sake

Computer virus writing is an art form. It can be very complex and coders can use very clever techniques to ply their trade, but consider the *Trojan* for a moment. Have you considered that any *warez* program could have *Trojan* code in it like Net*Bus*? Consider further, what if commercial licensed software was designed to include *Trojans*? A bit far fetched? Not really. Several of *Microsoft's* products have sort of Trojans in them.

Rumour

It was reported in a popular computer magazine that the beta release of Borland's C++ Builder v5 allegedly had a picture hidden in it of a dinosaur eating Bill Gates!

Harmless *Trojans* of this sort are known as *Easter Eggs.* Lots of programs, particularly games, contain them, though they are notoriously difficult to find.

Generally Easter Eggs are pretty boring stuff. They are the professional equivalent of hacker/cracker greetings messages. Most consist of hidden messages from the programmers but on rare occasions you'll find a very simple game or some such thing. One of the more interesting Easter Eggs was in the Lucas Arts game "Day Of The Tentacle" which was also known as "Manic Mansion II". In one of the rooms of this graphic adventure was a computer. When this computer was activated it was possible to play a copy of "Manic Mansion". Players thought that this was a nice touch, not realising that it was not fancy coding used to simulate extremely old blocky graphics and bad animation. The main game had simply shelled out to a copy of the original game, which was included with the new one.

Now, what would happen if a disgruntled coder inserted a potentially harmful, well-hidden and even encrypted code into a commercial piece of software that had a wide existing user base?

Word 2000 Easter Eggs

Here are some examples to try out if you have Word 2000.

1. In any document type "=rand(4,5)" and hit return. It will insert several lines saying "The quick brown fox jumps over the lazy dog."
2. In any document, press the ctrl, Alt and + sign at the same time. Your cursor will turn into a clover leaf (repeat to reverse).
3. In Office Assistant, type "cast" and click on the graphic.

The *Trojan* could be activated by a key known only to the coder and used as a method of blackmail.

For example, a bank manager gets a message that states a Scammer wants ten million to be deposited in a Swiss bank account or he will release a software key into the banking system which will cause all *Automatic Teller Machines* (*ATM)* to give out twice the requested money and not deduct it from the account. To show good faith the Scammer tells the bank manager that a certain *ATM* in the high street will be hit at a certain time.

Techniques like this work only because institutions like banks do not want anyone to know how insecure their systems actually are. This goes on a lot more often than anyone realises and the banks sometimes have no choice but to pay up.

Next time you read in the press about a bank's system or *ATM* machines going a bit strange, think about it laterally and read between the lines. Sometimes, that's the best place to look.

Spot the Hoax

"A deadly new computer virus that actually causes home computers to explode in a blast of glass fragments and flame has injured at least 50 people and killed at least one.

This virus cannot be detected. It does something to the computer's hardware, creating conditions that lead to dangerous short circuits and power surges.

The virus, unnamed as yet, was discovered in the UK by a college student when he was permanently blinded in one eye when his monitor exploded in his face.

How do you protect yourself? You either stop using the Internet or you take risks and hope that it would not happen to you..."

Email of unknown origin.

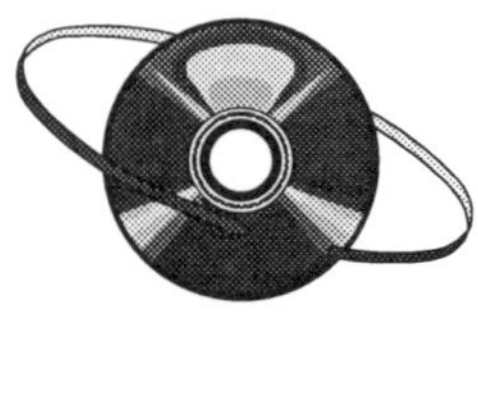

Chapter Ten

Protecting Your Information

"This was astonishing information..."
- Thomas Hardy

Information is what cyberspace is all about and what people often try hard to hide, but there are ways and means of acquiring it using unconventional methods.

For example, don't assume that your website is secure, just because the homepage needs a password before access to the rest of the site can be achieved. It isn't secure.

The Scammer can get in if they know what the pages are called. The easiest way to do that is by guessing. Alternately, if guessing doesn't work, the Scammer will go to a search engine and submit the website to be hacked as if it was their own site. After a few days or weeks the site will be indexed in the search engine. Amongst the information made public will be a list of the site's page names. The Scammer can now go there by just typing the address into their browser. This doesn't always work, as there are many security products on the market that are designed to prevent this very thing from happening. If you want to protect parts of your website from prying eyes, you will need to invest in some.

Do not underestimate the security risk your real-life garbage can pose either. A Scammer will sometimes go through the trash to see if they can discover any information about their target. Utilising this method is known as *'trashing'*.

Useful documents might include itemised phone bills, credit card receipts, photographs, personal documents or, indeed, anything that could be used for blackmailing purposes. It is *not* unusual for hackers and fone phreaks to go through the garbage of phone companies, colleges or other Information Technology based companies.

A lot of information on individuals and companies is available freely from public sources such as the voting register, telephone books and publicly available company records. Specialist software databases exist that contain the addresses and phone numbers of just about all *UK* citizens.

Using these sources, the Scammer can get more than three quarters of the information that is available on their target. Of the remaining information, most of it can be surmised from that already obtained.

Very little information is completely inaccessible to those who have knowledge of a few well-known techniques. As an example, take a look at the list below. How would you get this information? I swear that *every* single one of these names are *genuine* people who live in the *UK*.

Barbara Bottom	- There are literally hundreds of Bottoms in the UK.
Bill Gates	- There are 56 of them.
Dawn French	- There are 51 of them.
Fred West	- There are 200 of them.
Gillian Anderson	- There are 281 of them.
James Bond	- There are 213 of them.
John Brown	- After I got to 5,000 I stopped counting.
Margaret Thatcher	- There are 37 of them.
Pamela Anderson	- There are 253 of them.
Peter Stringfellow	- There are 15 of them.
Peter Sutcliffe	- There are 131 of them.
Rab Nesbitt	- There are 79 of them six of which have the middle initial C.
Allan Bastard	- There are 46 Bastards in the UK.
Richard Branson	- Unlucky for some, 13 of them.
Stephen King	- There are 999 of them (I thought it would be 666).
Tina Turner	- There are 105 of them.
Tony Blair	- Five of them.

And as if that lot wasn't bad enough, there is at least one *Anus* living in *London* at the moment. To preserve their dignity, I'll not reveal their Christian name (besides it's not funny enough).

Jim's the Name

When it comes down to it, the Internet is primarily two entities: a communication medium and an information repository.

The big problem with all this data is a lack of formal or abstract structure. The structure - if any - is more chaotic than anything else. Nevertheless, if you want information hard enough and put in the hours, it is staggering just what can be found out.

All searches start with the humble search engine. Top choices (out of tens of thousands) are those provided by *Yahoo, Lycos, Excite* and their ilk. Then there are the UseNet search engines like the one at *DejaNews*. These are excellent tools in their own right, but have been superseded to a large extent by the meta-engines. These link several search engines together and display the results in an (attempted) structured manner. The meta-engine at *www.google.com* is probably the best search tool currently on the whole planet.

A while back, I was bored (this is a bad sign - the devil finds work for idle hands and all that) so I decided to do a search on a friend of mine who lives in England. We will call him Jim (because that is his real name) and he's in the electronics trade.

A meta-search on his name turned up several thousand references. A few searches within these initial results for the words "United Kingdom", "England" and "UK" turned up a few hundred hits. That's still too many to render any useful information.

DejaNews turned up about 50 UseNet postings of that name. Just 18 of them turned out to be related to the Jim that I was looking for. A couple of them mentioned his company name.

Back to the meta-search using his name and (now) company details. Bingo! The main branch office in the USA had a listing of all their branches including two in England. Jim's email address was listed along with the company address, phone number and lots of other stuff.

I threw his email address into *Bigfoot, Yahoo* and *SavvySearch's* people finders and ended up with his town and postcode. This was enough to put into an online telephone directory (there are many) and get his full address and telephone number.

Armed with these details, I paid *Equifax's* online resources a visit. For a few pounds it would be possible to get a copy of Jim's credit history (which I decided not to do) which would even contain details of times when he had paid late or defaulted on credit re-payments.

The voting register was a bit of a damp squib. Some information was available on payment of a fee by credit card, but mostly you had to go round and pay the personal offices a visit. The same was true for the Census people and the registrars of Births, Deaths and Marriages. Nevertheless, I managed to find a lot of this stuff on a USA website. Once registered, I was allowed to make up to ten free searches a month.

Losing It

If securing information can be a concern so can getting rid of it. Any documents that are deleted may still remain in the form of copies stored in temporary files or inside the Windows swap file. These files would have to be deleted too.

This is not of much help. When a file is deleted it actually is still there (and can be undeleted) only it is hidden and the space it occupies is marked as available. The only way to be sure that the file is gone for good is to write other data over it.

PGP and other programs will do this. The military standard for hard drive 'washing' specifies that the file is written over at least seven times with random information (or carefully chosen patterns).

If the information is very sensitive the hard drive is also formatted (and can still be unformatted) and then finally put in a blast furnace to be melted down and recycled as chastity belts.

A few minutes search found a press cuttings agency that would (for a large fee) search their massive archives for information about anyone with that name. Or, if I actually knew details of any press stories about Jim, I could order photocopies online for a small fee from the *British Library*.

This was all very interesting, but yet I had just touched on the surface of what it was possible to find out. There was a massive amount of Internet resources still left to be explored.

At that point, I stopped my search. Further progress would have been tedious and bordering on the obsessive. Had I felt the need to continue (and been of a criminal personality), it would have been far easier to phone the likes of the DVLA, and the DHS and do a bit of creative social engineering.

Come to think of it, a close friend of mine worked for a private detective agency for over six years. She is still friendly with a few policemen. Do you think that that she could? Naaa! This is just getting silly! Oh my, I'm getting bored again...

Passwords

"A phrase is born into the world both good and bad at the same time. The secret lies in a slight, an almost invisible twist. The lever should rest in your hand, getting warm, and you can only turn it once, not twice."
- Issac Babel

Take care when choosing passwords. They are your *first* line of defence. If they are compromised it can lead to all sorts of undesirable events.

When choosing a password do *not* pick a subject that is closely connected with you. For example, if I was trying to break into your account and I discovered that you were a *Trekkie* then I would be trying to use passwords like these.

Picard, Kirk, Spock, McCoy, Bones,
Worf, Enterprise, Voyager, Crusher, DS9,
Quark, Borg, Janeway, etc.

If you were the boss of a company I would try these.

Topdog, Bossman, Highflyer,
Topcat, Bosscat, etc.

Some of the most common passwords are birthdays, family names, pet names and *CB* handles. All sexual words and general profanity are popular as passwords. Some *very* common passwords are.

Qwerty, Fred, Password,
123456789, Sysop and Billgates.

Hackers in particular compile enormous **common word lists** that they use to crack an account using an automated password-cracking tool. Choosing something that isn't connected with you creates a good password.

For example I do not like sport so a good password for me would be 'tennis'. To enhance the effectiveness of this password at least one non-alphabetical character should be added like this.

tennis7
%tennis%
ten+nis
t$ennis424

Using this method, even a password using as few as four characters can have several *million* possible combinations.

Becoming more prevalent are 'passphrases'. These are just very long passwords in the form of a sentence, perhaps picked randomly from a newspaper at random. Passwords should be changed periodically so that if your account *has* been secretly compromised the Scammer will have to start again from scratch after the password has been changed.

Do *not* use the same password for several different things. I know of one system operator (*Paul*) that used the same password all the time. One day, a user dialled into his system and tried to use *Paul's* own user *ID* and password to logon as a super-user and gain root access. This meant that the Scammer *must* have been running their own system and that *Paul* had visited it at some time using the same password as his own system. Luckily for *Paul*, he had finally implemented the above advice only the previous day (very lucky) and changed his system password. You can be sure he will not be caught out so easily again.

Encryption

"...I have been looking for him for the last two hours in vain. Where is he hiding?"
- From the Earth to the Moon, Jules Verne

In cyberspace there are widely available utilities that will let the Scammer (and the non Scammer) encrypt their emails, hard disks, directories and files.

These programs can be tens of thousands of times more secure than the *World War II ENIGMA* code.

Without a doubt the most popular and widely available is *Pretty Good Privacy (PGP).*

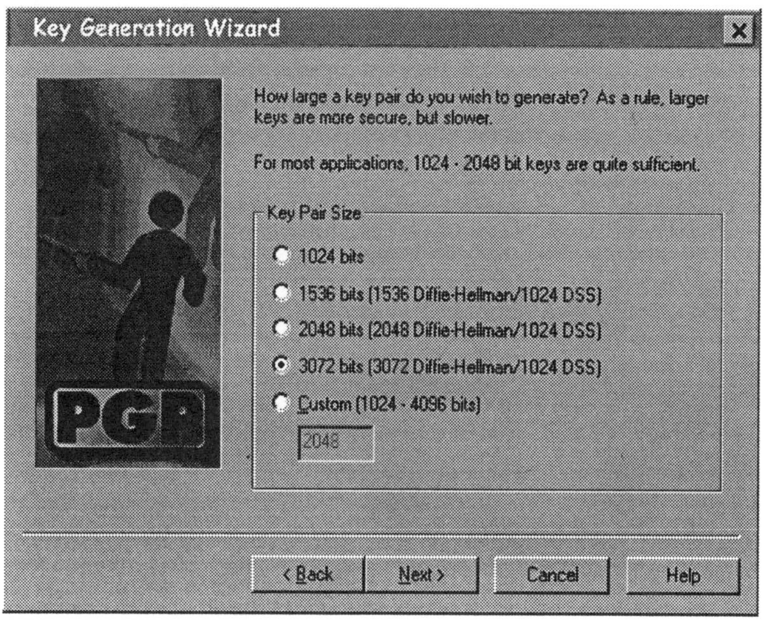

This program is one of the oldest encryption programs about and was the first to utilise (and invent) the concept of *Public* and *Private* encryption keys.

A *Public* encryption key is a cipher that is freely given out by the owner so that people will be able to send them secure information. Once encrypted, using the *Public* key, there is no known way of reading the information unless the recipient has a copy of the *Private* key.

Public keys can be left on the *PGP* sever for anyone to use. Information can be encrypted to several keys at the same time.

There is one disadvantage to using this method of encryption. Take a look at this message.

This is a test of encryption.

Now look at the *same* message after it has been encrypted.

```
----BEGIN PGP MESSAGE----
Version: PGP Personal Privacy 6.5.3

qANjR1DBwU4DK2NRBr5GRaEQCADoCgF9SsVPk/Ib0Af5/lwK
EezTU03btCL/I6DLjptKe5QoQ/Fa0gJFddROLj8Km1DhzIYx
WW2a747yYhgc+spZFjBUmzstBA/iSgG8L/zJ0iMS7RjdUiSY
qo1hRSb0HvHqpRo/9M8nChbENMl5iiBR7hrR2dY1HO447kDl
hNCIRcAmpyrpJ003tlZxVv7b8r7iit32ea+y59CLtFyABc0C
42ngsNL0LcZiHADPmTDcpYiOlRQkYeiZBtiNpygRdGQXQIOh
3FZFkenVMi08IpPXBW6EhABgCik38SEoQwm6xTsuwyDgmpP1
DYkFzjU42axtVs8Z6stDvCjvy6JHJKW1CACyj+jDKRNHgulO
lbsogAShXwKcN526Zzp9FfEsblcBCFaOsap5mlL8t3LzOS9e
x5RAUxfZfWM2gtwRSLtOin90HhFLC5L5lS4w5fqKblap2GCI
frZlrWya3WB7t9CYMmQWGBK9RIMpwQH2fe+zRYDFyGPPLx5a
eqGOloNfS05/MmIQ5C4X+1VUrtpKlioxMQ2CWLcGhOmnd0k7
ak47j1VX7/EdX+hoKSEy8UtHyxXYBrUhbP6OTCKACVv92l2c
4wsaMmSBEF7fLJAWevEKtMW7xQyUR87VzG0uoj1wfGeuNUPA
VfmOlbPrligiJKWupannf8jObKC7GBpI53ASsW0gyTQyiWPs
c617988ICJoWHXPjT83NIBuaTYXW/sq0+M4JWAhuyuwjQ9P1
Wnq6RLwINvQt1231XhX0
----END PGP MESSAGE----
```

The message which started off as only *29* characters long ends up a whopping *876* characters long as part of the complex encryption key is stored within it. You can see how an email of only a few pages will end up extremely long.

The information is very secure indeed, but you must make sure that the *Private* encryption key doesn't get lost or you are up the proverbial creek without a certain implement.

In the summer of *2000* the infamous *RIP Bill* was passed by the *House of Commons* and became the *RIP ACT*. It became illegal from that date to use encryption technology in the *UK* unless a copy of the *private* encryption key is deposited with the government on request.

Those Who Watch can now monitor your private email anytime they feel like it whether or not you are suspected of criminal activities.

If you encrypt something and then claim to have lost the password or decryption key you can be imprisoned for up to two years. If you tell anyone that the government has demanded a copy of your encryption key you can go to jail for up to four years.

Big Brother ***is*** watching you.

This *Act* enables law-enforcement powers to demand records of Internet traffic and view the content of encrypted messages. The actual implementation of this Bill did not take effect until *October* 2000. The snooping will be overseen from a multimillion-pound spy centre located within the headquarters of *MI5*.

Internet Service Providers are required by law to set up secure channels to the centre innocuously named as the *Government Technical Assistance Centre* so they can pass on information about Internet traffic.

The government was reputed to have contributed at least £*20* million to service providers to cover the initial cost of installing the links to the spy centre.

When you mention encryption there is always someone who will say, *"If you need encryption you must be up to no good."* To the non-user the only possible use of encryption are to help child pornographers and drug dealers evade detection. This is obviously nonsense!

There are simply masses of legitimate reasons to use encryption. Hackers often break into email servers. How would you like a very personal document stolen and posted for all to see in a newsgroup?

Maybe you are a doctor passing sensitive medical details on to a specialist? Even if your email is innocent in content it could still be embarrassing to have it disclosed in a public place.

Don't you think that the individual has the right to privacy regardless of the medium? A lot of people don't think so, but if the government started opening their letters and parcels just to have a look in case they were up to anything, they would soon kick up a fuss. It's a classic case of 'not in my back yard'.

In many people's humble opinion the *RIP Act* is a waste of time. To the Scammer the *RIP Act* is just a very slight pain in their massively muscular backside. Probably more than *99.99* percent of email is used for non-criminal purposes and will bore *those who watch* to death.

As for criminal activities, information can be hidden in an email so that it cannot be seen. The art of concealing information is known as *Stenanography.* Programs already exist on the Internet that will do this job for you.

One such program hides the information within a picture file. A side effect of this is that the picture loses some quality, but it is not as noticeable with black and white images.

An easier way to hide information inside a picture file (in a manner that doesn't degrade quality) is with the *DOS* copy command.

```
copy /b oldpicture.jpg+message.txt newpicture.jpg
```

To view the message you would just load the picture file into *Windows* notepad. There would be gobbledygook shown at the beginning of the file, but it would not affect the message. The picture file can still be viewed as normal.

Technically the *RIP Act* has not been violated, as the message has *not* been encrypted. If the sender was sufficiently paranoid they could encrypt the message first. Then put it in a password protected archive and finally *hide* it inside a picture.

Files can be encrypted as well as email. One of the safest file encryption algorithms in regular use is known as *Blowfish.* Its source code is public domain and its encryption algorithm is stronger than the government's own *Data Encryption Standard* (*DES*).

With the use of a device driver, a directory or your entire hard drive can be secured with *Blowfish*. In *1997* a *DES* encrypted file was cracked by a group of students using thousands of computers linked together. *Blowfish* is reputed to have *never* been cracked (though after seeing what is needed just to crack *DES*, it seems unlikely than anyone will even bother trying).

An alternative to encrypting the whole hard drive is to create an encrypted virtual drive. This is one big encrypted file that simulates a hard drive. It is only accessible after using a passphrase.

Chat

"Knowledge is of two kinds. We know a subject ourselves, or we know where we can find information upon it..."
- Samuel Johnson

Internet Relay Chat (IRC) can be a good resource for finding and sharing information. It's a place for the would be hacker to swap techniques or (in normal chat rooms) to *phish* for information.

Gone Phishing

Phish, is hacker speak for fish.

A lot of their jargon is deliberately misspelled. Words like *kewl, phreak, phuk* and *fone* are trendy. Not so popular these days is the strange practice of writing text in AlTeRnAtInG upper and lower case. I guess they must have finally realised at last how irritating and unreadable this is.

Another irritating thing that is very much in vogue at the moment in hacker chat rooms is the use of weird unreadable nicknames that have a hidden meanings. For example, the nickname 5469676779 (pure hex notation) is hexadecimal for Tiggy. So is 0x840x1050x1030x1030x121 (C++ notation).

IRC is the infamous set of *Internet* chat rooms that are often reported about in the media as an increasing cause of marriage break-ups and stalking.

I hadn't been in a hacker chat room for months, but ***just for you***, I paid a visit to **#2600uk** located on the **uk.undernet.org** server. I pretended to be a beginner and asked a newbies question.

"Why is this chat room called #2600uk?"

You'll remember that *2600hz* is the frequency that *USA Fone Phreaks* use to take control of a line when they steal free calls. In the *UK* the frequency is *2280hz.* I was actually curious to find out why the room was called **#2600uk** and not **#2280uk**.

Well, you would have though I had shot *Bambi!* I got extreme abuse back and was told several things about my mother that I did not want to know! I hope that they are not true, but if they are, I did not realize that the old dear still had it in her (or was so open minded).

After a few minutes *someone* requested a private chat. During the course of it, I was to be told about a reputed backdoor in one of the more reputable firewalls and how to use it.

A *backdoor* is secret way into a program or system that the programmer uses for testing purposes (or with the intension of using the *backdoor* to break in themselves). It is supposed to be removed after the final program is released, but often isn't.

Social Engineering

"I think you are a very bad man," said Dorothy.
- L. Frank Baum, The Wonderful Wizard Of Oz

Social Engineering is just a modern word for manipulating or conning people. It is the third oldest profession (spying is second and prostitution first) known to mankind. People such as police, teachers and salesmen are actually taught *Social Engineering* techniques when they are educated for their job.

The first time I became aware of *Socially Engineering* was when I was 12 years old. I was such an eccentric kid that they sent me to a child psychologist. During the interview, I was asked if I sometimes told lies. I was so staggered by the implications of this questions that I struggled hard not to laugh. Even at 12 I realised that a liar would have answered *"No"* whilst an honest person would have said *"Yes"*. Guess what answer I gave?

The psychologist had just been *Socially Engineered.*

The ability to tell straight-faced lies is a major survival technique that most people (including me) never develop. The best way to tell lies is by actually telling the truth in such a way that it is not believed.

In a *con* involving the sending of emails there are no body-language signs to warn the victim off. No nervous twitching, no sweating, no stammering, no lack of eye contact. There is simply time for unanticipated reactions to be manipulated.

The cyberspace Scammer will sometimes have to make a more direct contact with their victim. For this, a rehearsal pays off. If the contact happens over the phone, the Scammer can prepare a list of answers to anticipated awkward questions.

Here is how they might try and manipulate their victim into giving out a password over the phone.

> *"Hello, this is John from Network support. Who am I talking too?"*
>
> *"Joe Bloggs.""Hi Joe. Not seen you in ages. How's things? We've been having a bit of bother with the Network. Have you been having any problems logging into the system?"*
>
> *"No? None at all. Seems just the same as usual."*
>
> *"I better run a check. Just keying up your details now. Do you have a long password or a short one?"*
>
> *"A short one."*
>
> *"Ah, that is why you've not had any problems. It only seems to be affecting the more complicated passwords. Ah, here is your details. Just hold on a second while I check your logon."*

A short silence follows...

"Nope! Can't logon. It's the same error message as the others. Your password isn't being verified."

"It was okay this morning?"

"Maybe the spelling or case in our records is wrong? Could you please spell it for me?"

"All uppercase. T. I. N. K. E. R."

"That's what we've got on file. Wonder why it's not working?" Oh, it's accepting it now. Must have been a typo on my part. Thanks for your help. I better go 'cause I've got loads more to check. Bye!"

And the victim never suspects for a moment that *John* is actually a *15*-year-old computer hacker with a deep voice looking for a way into the company's computer system.

It can be surprising how much information gleaned from people by just asking a polite direct question. Telesales operatives do it all the time. You've probably had loads of phone calls that start, *"Do you rent a video recorder or TV?"* or *"How much was your last phone bill?"* No attempt is made at deception. Even canvassers at the door do it, *"Excuse me, but are you the householder?"* Surprisingly enough, most people will just answer intrusive questions like this automatically without even considering the questioner's motives.

Old-fashioned *cons* like the *chain letter* have gained new life in cyberspace. Instead of the creator sending out dozens of letters, they can send out thousands of emails at a time with very little cost. They have become very sophisticated and convincing. Take a look at this:

Make $10,000 US cash in the next two weeks:

There are three addresses listed below. Send the person at the top of the list a $5 bill wrapped in two pieces of paper (to securely hide it), along with a note that says: "Please add me to your mailing list".

Then delete that name, move the other two up and put your name at the bottom.

Now start sending this ENTIRE email back out to people. When 20 people receive it, those 20 people will move your name up to the middle position and they will each send out 20. That totals 400 people that will receive this letter with your name in the middle.

Then, those 400 people will move your name up to the top and they will each send out 20 Emails. That totals 8,000 people that will receive this Email with your name at the top and they will each send you a $5 bill.

8,000 people each sending you a $5 bill = $40,000 cash. That's if everyone responds to this Email, but not everyone will, so you can expect more realistically to receive about $10,000 cash in $5 bills in your mailbox.

This will work for anyone, anywhere in the world in any country, but send only a US CASH $5 bill.

The more Emails you send out, the more cash you will receive. If each person sends out 100 Emails, there will be 1,000,000 people that receive this letter when your name reaches the top. If only 1% of those people respond, you will still get $50,000 cash.

1.Regan Reaney - Canada
2.Tina Vemb - Canada
3.Lillian Meyer - Canada

When your name reaches the top in a few days, you will start receiving $5 bills from other people just like yourself, who are willing to invest a $5 bill to receive $10,000 cash."

There is nothing that motivates people more than money for nothing and cheques for free. Perhaps you wouldn't fall for it (would you), but plenty do.

The 'King' of the *Social Engineers* is the paedophile. These twisted individuals are usually found hanging about in kiddie chat rooms pretending to be a youngster themselves (or a sympathetic young adult).

They are skilled at getting information out of kids (*phishing*) and can manipulate them into hiding details of their new "*friend*" from their parents. They will often take months to strike up an empathy with their victims. When the trust has been developed they will only then suggest a meeting. They are also *very* cautious people because they know that some adults try to fool paedophiles into thinking they are also kids so that they can entrap them.

Think twice about letting your kids use a chat room unsupervised. In fact, anyone who uses chat rooms on the Net should be a bit cautious about the people they converse with.

A popular pastime in chat rooms is that of ordinary people pretending to be what they are not (though not usually for malicious reasons). Men pretend to be women. Women pretend to be men. Kids pretend to be adults. The anti-establishment pretend to be pro-establishment in order to infiltrate the enemy. Straights pretend to be gay and vice-versa. Whilst most people *aren't* out to get you, *some* people are out to get *anyone* at all.

There *are* some right weirdoes out there. A little paranoia can go a *long* way.

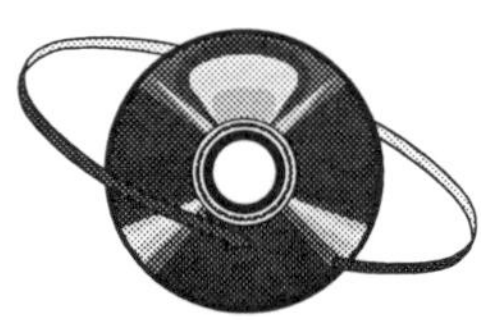

Chapter Eleven

Improve Your Online Security

"There is something that Governments care far more for than human life, and that is the security of property, and so it is through property that we shall strike the enemy..."
- Emmeline Pankhurst

Some do's and don'ts to improve your own online security and to help protect yourself from Internet scammers...

Don't...

use a credit/debit card online unless it is with reputable company that uses a securely encrypted/protected server. A lot of e-companies will let you order goods online and then let you phone your card details in later. And remember; just because your browser says that it is a secure site doesn't necessarily mean that it is. It could be just a message box supplied by the Scammer's website meant to make you *think* it is a secure server.

Do...

change the file names of the two most dangerous *DOS* programs that come free with *Windows*. *FDISK.EXE* and *FORMAT.EXE*. Trojans or compiled batch files sometimes call one (or both) of these programs in order to wipe the entire contents of the hard drive.

Both programs require the input of a user to answer yes or no before they will act. It is very easy for the Scammer to create a sample text file containing the keystrokes and send it into *FORMAT* or *FDISK* as a *YES* instruction.

Another dangerous *DOS* program that can also wipe the whole hard drive is *DELTREE.EXE.* Rename it as well.

Alternately, remove the programs altogether, but remember to keep a copy on a bootable disk.

✔

Do...

use anti-virus software. Go for one that includes an email scanner and offers free updates from the web. I recommend *McAfee* anti-virus. It is inexpensive and its free virus data updates come out weekly and during emergencies.

Remember virus-killing software is only as good as its data files, so if an upgrade is offered weekly then get one weekly. Dozens (sometimes hundreds) of new viruses appear every week.

✔

Do...

use a firewall. A good one (and free for personal use) is called *ZoneAlarm.* If you are regularly connected to the Internet for more than a few minutes at a time you *are* in danger from the cyber Scammer. *McAfee's Firewall* is also very good, but it isn't *freeware.* If you are really worried you can use two different *firewalls.*

✔

Do...

use a *Spam Trap.* If using *UseNet,* include it in an email address that you can afford to dispose of if you get attacked with malicious email or mail bombed. You don't even need to offend anyone for this to happen. Sometimes you are just a random target. Set up a free pop (offline) email account at **www.hotmail.com** or **www.yahoo.com** or use a mail forwarding system like that found at **www.bigfoot.com** to post your email on to your regular address.

Don't...

make assumptions about emails. More and more relationships are being tested because of a certain type of spam. I'm talking about unsolicited pornographic mail. There are a dozen ways in which emails can be obtained. If you are looking in the deleted folder one day and see loads of pornographic newsletters and adverts, do not judge your partner too harshly. It is unlikely that they have joined this type of mailing list but that they have been spammed.

The typical unsolicited pornozine will nearly always use profanity to get the message across (the legitimate ones do not). Sometimes there is a *"sample"* photo attached to the mail and always a link to go to for more free samples. Un-welcomed mail like this is best ignored. Unfortunately, you cannot use a mail filter on them to send them straight to the trash folder as they constantly change their email origin address and the subject line. The addresses on the links will be disguised by using the IP address instead of an URL so that the average person would not know which host to complain to. A minute with a whois/finger client will usually sort this out.

Do not make the mistake of falling for their *"To Be Removed From Our Mailing List Click This Link"*. They do not have a mailing list as such so you cannot leave it. If you click on that link you will just end up on their website which is where they wanted you to go to in the first place. Worse still, you will be confirming that the address they *harvested* from a newsgroup (or from wherever they obtained it) is a live address and you'll get even more such spam.

There is also no point in trying to reply to these emails as the replies are never collected. They know that they will get thousands of complaints. The return address will either not be in use, a fake or the address of a poor unsuspecting individual or company – again harvested from a newsgroup. Annoying as they maybe, all you can really do with this kind of mail is to completely ignore it. It usually stops after a few weeks.

Don't...

EVER give out a password to anyone on the Net or phone - even if it is someone you 'know'. It might not be them and it could be a Scammer socially engineering you. If you are ever disposing of old documents that include details of passwords, credit cards (or *any* personal information) burn them or (if there is nowhere you can safely burn them) at least rip them up into small bits.

The dog ate my homework might not be a *good* excuse in school, but it *is* a good way to dispose of documents.

Don't...

respond to *trolls* in *anyway whatsoever.* When you realise what is going on simply post a polite message to the other users of the newsgroup urging that they do not respond to the *troll* either. *Trolls* love attention.

Do not discuss the *troll* with other group members. The more you mention them, the longer they will stay. The more abuse that is directed toward them the happier they will become.

The worse thing you can do to a *troll* is to totally ignore him/her/it. It is recommended that you use your newsreader's built in mail-filters (also known as a killfile) to send messages from the *troll* straight to an *undesirable's* folder or, better still, delete it sight unread.

Don't...

give out personal information unless you know the motives of the requester. Be particularly careful in chat rooms. They are public places and you could end up with a stalker.

It's safer to use the international chat rooms than the local ones, because if you end up talking to a nutter they are less likely to turn up at your front door if they live thousands of miles away.

If the opportunity is available, always use a nickname or handle. If you inadvertently offend someone, apologise, particularly when in hacker forums or chat rooms. They are the last people you would want to offend.

Don't...

ever post your address or phone number in a newsgroup and be wary of anyone else who does.

This might seem like an obvious piece of common sense information, but I've seen it done on several occasions. Sometimes it is done without thinking. Other times, it has been done by a Scammer wishing to cause problems for the true owner of the address or phone number.

Don't...

criticise people's grammar, spelling or typographical mistakes when in chat rooms or *Newsgroups*. This is considered extremely bad manners and may result in an attack on you.

Also be careful of typing everything in capital letters as it's considered *SHOUTING*! Posting to Newsgroups in *Hyper-Text Markup Language (HTML)* is also considered bad manners and will get you flamed.

Don't...

let your kids surf the web unsupervised. It is too easy to accidentally connect up to pornographic websites. A lot of these sites deliberately use Meta tags such as *MP3, Britney Spears* or whichever celebrity happens to be popular at the time.

Search engines' spiders find these sites and index them as a music or celebrity site etc and the kiddies get one big shock when they go there looking for the latest pictures of *Robbie Williams.*

You can greatly reduce the chances of this happening by using one of the website censorship programs like *Cybersitter, Netnanny* or their ilk. If you do let the kids surf by themselves then this is a *must.*

For the really paranoid newsgroup user, find the list of Newsgroups available (it will be on your hard drive somewhere) and edit the undesirables out of it using word pad or a word processor that can save in *ASCII* format - the groups will usually be listed in a text file called something like *GROUPS.DAT.*

Do...

take a little time to examine your own headers from your own newsgroup postings. Is there anything in them that you don't want others to know? If so, you will have to do a bit of hacking of your newsreader software.

Do your *ISP* account details show up in the header? If so your disposable email address isn't safe. Some newsreader software programmes use the owner's *ISP* logon *ID* as an *ID* for messages. For a lot of folk this *ID* is also your email address.

The headers shown earlier were pretty basic and are included in just about all newsreaders. Here is an example of just how much information some newsreaders can add to the postings.

Article: 2502 of alt.cyberspace.test
Path: goats-tooth.cyberspace.net!not-for-mail
From: slabber@bachel.com (Mister Slabber)
Newsgroups: alt.cyberspace.test
Subject: Test Message
Date: Mon, 7 Aug 2002 15:27 +0100 (BST)
Organization: Cyberspace Internet Service Unlimited Limited
Lines: 12
Sender: *@modem-37.thevitalspark.dialup.pol.co.uk
Message-ID: <8muh0lgrs1@goats-tooth.cyberspace.net>
Reply-To: slabber@bachel.com
NNTP-Posting-Host: modem-37.thevitalspark.dialup.pol.co.uk
X-Trace: goats-tooth.cyberspace.net 12.136.56.37 (7 Aug 2002 14:27:33 GMT)
X-Complaints-To: abuse@cyberspace.net

NNTP-Posting-Date: 7 Aug 2002 14:27:33 GMT
Xref: goats-tooth.cyberspace.net
cyberspace.cyberspace.test:2450
Xreader: Vinculum v1.01 expired - you must register now!

In addition to all this, it is also possible to automatically add your own headers to all out going messages.

✔

Do...
take extra care protecting your kids from pornography. As said earlier on in the book, sometimes the viewer is tricked into visiting these abhorrent sites. Remember, if you do see something offensive by accident it will already be on your hard disk drive.
To get rid of this type of thing you have to shut down your browser and delete the contents of the Temp Internet directory. It is also a good idea to delete the contents of the normal Temp directory.
Do not forget to empty the Recycle Bin as this offensive material will not actually have been deleted, but just moved into the Recycle Bin.
Copies may also be stored inside the Windows swap file, which you will need to set to zero (percent of your hard drive) in order to empty it properly.
The same accidental visit will also have been recorded in the browser History that means that any nosey kid could also click on it. Get rid of that too.
Finally, remember that deleted files can often be recovered so do not underestimate the intelligence of your ten year old or their obsessive curiosity.

✔

Do...
use a text only mail/news reader. You are only safe from email attacks if you use a non-HTML email/news reader. Even then, beware of file attachments. Make it common practice not to run an executable file or program script unless it is from someone you know well (it should be scanned first anyway).

Do...

send sensitive emails using an encryption program like *Pretty Good Privacy* (*PGP* is free for personal use). You don't know who could be looking at your mail on any of the many servers that it might be routed through on its way to its final destination. *Blackmail* is just as popular in cyberspace as in real life.

Don't...

use *ICQ's* homepage option. If you use *any* form of instant messenger then be vigilant as you are particularly vulnerable to social engineering (especially if you are male).

For example, if you are a normal hot-blooded male and a female has been flirting with you for ages over *ICQ*, the offer of seeing her photo is very tempting. The trouble is that the photo file she sends contains a *Trojan*. And *she* is really a *he*; a big fat skinhead with tattoos and body piercings.

Beware of reputed graphic files, which are named like *MyHouse.bmp.exe.* They may be graphic files, but they are also programmes that could do just about anything (see next *Don't*) whilst showing you the graphic.

Don't...

use *warez.* It really isn't worth the risk from viruses, *Trojans* and potentially malicious forms of *Spyware. Trojans* are easy to install into any piece of software. The Scammer just needs to join the Trojan file and the utility file together with a very small piece of code that enables both programs to run consecutively. The *Trojan* secretly installs itself before the main program is run. If the Scammer isn't a programmer, there are utilities available on the Internet, which will join the two files together and insert the code for them.

Do...

keep an eye on your modem lights. If the *OH* light is on then the phone line is off the hook. Some scammer software will dial-out to a high-call-charge overseas number without letting on.

If the *CD* light is on then your computer is connected to another computer. If you are online and not doing anything then the *RX* (receive - also known as *RD*) and the *TX* (transmit - also known as *TD*) lights should not be doing anything more than give the occasional weak flash. If they are flashing frequently, then something is accessing your system. If you have an internal modem, you will not have these lights, but you can get software that will display the same thing on your monitor. The popular firewall *Zonealarm* also shows all outgoing and incoming data flow whilst running in the system tray.

Do...

use a proxy server. If a password is the first line of defence then the proxy server is the second. Think of it as a stepping-stone (or relay) on the way to your *ISP's* server. Using one makes it harder to be traced.

The information contained in your message headers will not show your *ISP* information, but that of the proxy. Whenever you visit any website, there is the potential of your *ISP* information being recorded by that website. By using a proxy, that information is not available.

For the paranoid, it is possible to chain several proxies together (not easy) thus confusing the trail even further.

Do...

consider your cookies. These are small text files created by a lot of websites on your computer's hard drive. They hold information pertaining to that website, like your passwords, email address, how many visits you have made and other information.

If a Scammer gets into your system they can find out a lot about you by studying your cookies. It is a simple matter to go into your system's Internet setting and switch cookie support off.

Unfortunately some websites will not let you view them unless you accept a cookie from them. Cookies can also be of help as you don't need to type in the same information each time you visit that website.

You may like to consider a utility that deletes all or listed cookies automatically at system start or shut down. Such utilities usually have other benefits as they can include options such as deleting surfing history, deleting favourites, deleting recent documents and/or hiding system options such as using dangerous programs such as regedit, adding/deleting programs, hiding printer settings and lots of other options.

Don't...

leave a web cam or microphone plugged in when it is not in use. If a hacker compromises your system then they can use a web cam or microphone to observe and eavesdrop on you. They can take pictures and record what you are saying. It is another opportunity for blackmail.

Don't...

say anything on the telephone that you wouldn't feel comfortable saying in a loud voice in a crowded public place. You don't know who could be listening. A Cyber Scammer? A bored phone engineer or even *Big Brother?* Be particularly vigilant if you use an old fashioned style of analogue cordless handset.

After the Scammer finds a few such lines, a scanner is programmed to monitor them and will jump to a channel if it finds any traffic. Get yourself a digital cordless.

Do...

store your data on a *different* hard drive or partition. If you download something nasty and it mucks up your hard drive it will be far easier to fix if all your data files are on a different drive.

Do...

back-up drives regularly. Use a utility to copy a compressed drive image file onto another hard drive or partition. Then put this image on a *CDR/CDRW/ZIP* drive or a tape.

Not only will this save your data, but also it saves all the customisations of your software, which can take an awful long time to restore. Virus and *Trojan* attacks are on the increase.

Don't...

answer unsolicited telephone enquiries *unless* the caller's motives are readily apparent. When in doubt, deny everything or tell lies, *"Sorry, I got a luxury fitted kitchen/double glazing put in last week."* Ask the caller where they got your phone number from and ask it to be removed from their company's database. Consider getting an ex-directory number. The same goes for unsolicited mail.

Beware of the letter that tells you to phone a number to claim a prize you have won in a contest you didn't enter. This is social engineering in action. You have probably won a cheap pen and it will cost you a fortune in phone charges to find this out.

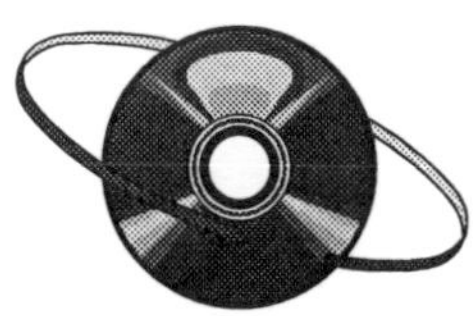

Last Word

"By the end of the day I had been called a lot of things and introduced to a whole new language..."
- Jack Trancer

Like it or not the cyber Scammer is here to stay. Though, as I guess you know by now, they ain't always the bad guys. With the recent introduction of devices like Wireless Application Protocol (WAP) mobiles, you are at an increasing risk each day.

With services being added to the *World Wide Web* on a daily basis, the system is becoming more and more filled with exploitable flaws. In any system, flaws must *exist*. It is the nature of systems to breed flaws. Entropy encourages it. Exploitation *will* occur. There has to be a Scammer and a Victim. Which one will you be?

If you take heed of the advice offered in this book your vulnerability to the cyber Scammer will be greatly reduced. To ignore the suggestions offered would be very foolish.

If you *stop* being a victim, the Scammer will move on to pastures new. The only way to avoid being a victim is by a process of awareness and of education. Ask questions. Listen. Observe. Poke your nose into places where it is not welcome. Stir things up. But most of all, spread the word...

You may think all possible cyber scams have already been perpetrated, but you'd be wrong. Appearing on the horizon is *Biometric* hacking. This is real science fiction stuff; hacking retinal scanners, fingerprint scanners and other exotic devices.

Already the most complex information system ever conceived is being hacked as we speak. It is called *Deoxyribonucleic Acid*

(*DNA*). The hackers are called genetic scientists. The program is the human genome.

This might seem as far way away from the Internet as you can get? Wrong. By the time you read this, the millions of words that make up·the map of the human genome should be available on the Internet free from *Project Gutenberg.* *DNA* is nothing more than an incredibly complex abstract data structure. Data is the Internet. Data is power. Data is all.

The gaps between hardware, software and organic technologies are merging. You can be sure that the hackers will be there to exploit the final "*final*" frontier. They in turn will themselves be exploited by a new type of Scammer. A type that we can never imagine. Exploiting science has become indistinguishable from magic.

It's really something to think about, isn't it?

Appendix A

Internet Scammer Jargon

ADC
Analogue to Digital Converter. An integral component of the modem. Found in hardware devices used to steal cable TV channels and satellite television.

Anti-Virus
Software used to track down, identify and prevent infection from computer viruses.

ASCII
American Standard Code for Information Interchange. The basic system for the exchange of data in text format. Also know as *"plain"* or *"vanilla"* text, it is available across all computer platforms.

Attack
Unwanted attentions from a scammer intent on exploiting you.

Back Door
A secret way into a program or system put there by the programmers.

BBS
Bulletin Board System. An automated piece of software that will answer the telephone and allow invited users to pass messages and files between them. Before the Internet, was the biggest resource of the software pirate.

Bomb
The sending of excessive amounts of data with the intent to either annoy the recipient or slow up a system to the point where it can no longer function. The latter is also known as a *Denial Of Services (DOS)* attack. A *"logic bomb"* is a Trojan program that will perform a particular function when a particular series of circumstances occur.

Carding
Credit/debit card crime. Also the manufacture of fake cards with real users' details added to them electronically. Adjusting and faking of data stored on such cards.

Chipping
Hardware hacking. Copying computer code from hardware chips. Altering such code and replacing it in a new computer chip.

CLI
Caller Line Identification. A code sent by the phone company that identifies the originator of the call.

Cracks
A crack is the term used for a small software *"patch"* (a program or script) which when operated upon the target software will add more functionality, remove copy protection or time limits. Such software is said to have been *"cracked"*.

Cracker
Code adjuster or protection remover. A person who cracks.

DAC
Digital to Analogue Converter. Just like an ADC in reverse.

Dilbert
Someone working in the field of Information Technology. From the popular cartoon strip of the same name.

Dongle
Hardware copyright protection device. Reputed to be the hardest method of copy protection to crack. Will usually be a small device which plugs into a computer's serial, parallel or Universal Serial Bus (USB) port.

DOS
Disk Operating System. The original sort of operating system on the IBM PC and clones. Often used as a general term for any environment which uses a command-line to execute commands. Not to be confused with the same acronym for *Denial Of Services.*

Encryption
Secure method of storing sensitive information. Everything within the encrypted environment - which can be a document, disk drive, email or others items - is effectively scrambled and needs a complex set of key codes, passwords or pass phrases in order to be accessible.

FAST
Federation Against Software Theft. Cyber cops who track down the purveyors and users of illegally copied and distributed software.

Firewall
A hardware or software device used to keep hackers out by either watching open computer ports for unscheduled activity and/or making sure that such open ports are either closed off or appear to be inaccessible.

Flame
To respond with a strong and/or defamatory retort. An unreasonable or extreme reaction to another's viewpoint.

Forum
Small collection of Newsgroups. Not part of UseNet, but similar in structure.

Forger
One who manufactures copies of software/hardware products, made to look like the genuine article in terms of packaging and functionality and attempts to pass off as such at a lower price.

Freeware
Free Software. Can be copied and distributed providing that the

creator is given credit and no fee is charged other than that of the storage media and a reasonable duplication charge.

Hacker
A cyber explorer and/or intruder. Also used by media in particular to mean any form of computer user who engages in criminal activity. Used by hackers to mean *"explorer"*.

Hacktivism
To hack for a higher cause. For patriotic reasons or for the righting of great wrongs. To 'free' individuals and societies from things such as exploitation, torture, oppression and slavery.

ICQ
I Seek You. A piece of Internet software that will automatically contact a central database server in order to see if your friends are online at the same time. Messages and files can be passed back and forth as can actual online chat. ICQ is the product name of the most popular item of software which does this.

IRC
Internet Relay Chat. The so-called infamous Internet chat rooms that the media are (mostly incorrectly) obsessed with as incredibly bad places full of hackers, perverts and home wreckers.

Lamer
Idiot (sometimes used to mean beginner). Extremely detrimental. Ironically often used by true lamers to describe anyone that they are trying to put down.

LAN
Local Area Networks. Several computers connected in such a way as to be able to share resources and exchange data.

LINUX
Freeware version of *UNIX*. Originally a command line environment like DOS, but now with an extremely flexible *Graphic User Interface* (*GUI*) called simply X (or X-Windows) to rival that of Microsoft Windows. A very stable multi-tasking environment.

Lurker
Someone who observes but does not participate. Also used to signify shyness and/or anti-social people.

MODEM
Modulator/Demodulator. A device containing a DAC and an ADC that allows a computer to talk to another computer or network. Basically the modem converts the digital computer signal into sound waves which are sent along the telephone line and converted at the other end back into digital computer codes.

Newbie
Beginner. Sometimes used detrimentally.

PGP
Pretty Good Privacy. The original software which set the standard for personal data security and encryption which, along the way, managed to greatly upset the US

government who did not want the public to have access to this technology.

Phreak
Originally used to mean someone who *"steals"* free phone calls. Is now a general term for someone who loves, and often exploits, telephone systems.

Port
Technically a place in computer memory where any device to the outside world (a peripheral) is located. In Internet terms, used to mean a place in the computer's memory which is capable of interfacing with the Internet. Nearly all ports are so designed for general purpose use, but some are assigned for specific purposes. For example, chat servers will often connect up to ports 6667 and 6668.

Pirate
Someone who blatantly sells illegally copied software for personal monetary gain. Often used by organised criminals as an easy way of fund raising for other activities.

Script Kiddie
Lamer who uses hacker tutorials to vandalise. Also extremely insulting term to real hackers.

Shareware
Try before you buy software. Similar to Freeware, but either with a time limit on it or limited functionality. Some Shareware is the fully working program with no time limits which, if liked or used regularly, relies on the users honesty to pay the registration fee.

Signature
A sequence of bytes that is typical of code-sections known to originate from a particular computer virus.

Sniffing
Searching or watching ports for packets of data which can then be copied or followed to their destination. Can also be traced back to their point of origin if the packet sniffer software is on the incoming port. Can be automated.

Spam
Unsolicited advertising email or posting. Spamming is considered extremely bad manners and perpetrators are sometimes dealt with harshly.

Spoofing
Faking. A general term used to refer to any method used by the hacker to hide their origins from cyber cops.

Stenanography
The art of hiding information within other data, such as sending someone a secret message contained within an otherwise normal-looking picture file.

Troll
Person who wanders from Newsgroup to Newsgroup deliberately upsetting people. Also general insult particularly aimed at the pedantic or argumentative.

Trojan
That which pretends to be something else. For example, a program that looks like a nice little game which, on playing, surreptitiously steals your passwords and emails them elsewhere.

UNIX
The operating system of most Internet servers. Now being increasingly replaced by LINUX systems. For some odd reason they are referred to as LINUX or UNIX boxes.

UseNet
Large collection of Newsgroups. A messaging system where enthusiasts swap messages or binaries (pictures, data or program files) in a publicly accessible place.

Virus
Self replicating computer code, intentionally coded usually with the intent of vandalism.

WAN
Wide Area Networks. Just like a Local Area Network (LAN), but connected over a larger physical distance usually with far more computers.

Warez
Illegal copies of software (usually cracked). Another name for the goods of software pirates.

Worm
A specific type of computer virus that spreads by email. Originally a general term to describe any computer virus that slows systems down by eating into their resources.

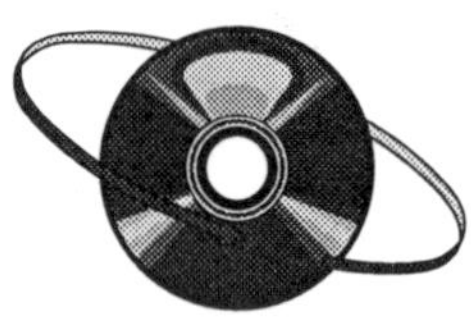

Appendix B

Internet Scammer/Anit-scammer Resources

E-Zines

2600	- General hacking and phreaking.
40hex	- Virus writing and protection.
Computer Underground Digest	- Security, news, social reports
Forbidden Knowledge	- Information on unusual subjects.
Phrack	- Hard core hacking.
SWAT	- Hack, Phreak, Virus, Anarchy and more.
The Crypt	- General underground news.

Publications

2600 Magazine	- By Lots of writers.
A Complete Hackers Handbook*	- By Dr-K.
Approaching Zero	- By Bryan Clough & Paul Mungo.
Hackers	- By Paul Taylor.
Hackers	- By Steve Levy.
Hacking Exposed	- By Stuart McClure.
Information Warfare *	- By Winn Schwartau.
Maximum Security	- By Anonymous.
Steal This Computer Book	- By Wallace Wang.
Surfing on the Internet	- By J. C. Herz.
The Hacker Crackdown *	- By Bruce Sterling.
The Hackers Handbook	- By Hugo Cornwall.
The Ralph Brown Interrupt List	- By *Guess Who!*

** Highly Recommended reading*

Newsgroups

alt.2600	- Info on hacking, cracking phreaking.
alt.binaries.e-book	- Information on books.
alt.binaries.cracks	- Software cracks and patches.
alt.binaries.hacking.utilities	- Hacking utilities.
alt.binaries.warez	- Information on software pirating.
alt.cellular	- Information on mobile phones.
alt.computer.security *	- Information on security.
alt.crime	- Information on crime.
alt.hackers	- Information on hacking.
alt.hackers.malicious	- Information on how to swear a lot.
alt.hacking	- Information on hacking.
alt.os.security	- Information on computer security.
alt.ph.uk *	- Info on hacking and phreaking in *UK.*
alt.phreaking	- Information on phone systems.
alt.security	- Information on security.
alt.security.espionage	- Information on espionage.
alt.security.pgp	- Information on encryption.
alt.security.terrorism	- Information on terrorism.
alt.society.anarchy	- Information on anarchy.
borland.public.cpp.language	- Programming C++.
borland.public.tasm	- Programming assembler.
borland.public.turbopascal	- Programming PASCAL.
free.phone-calls	- Info on getting free phone calls.

** Highly Recommended*

Useful URL's

http://packetstorm.securify.com *	- Security related resources.
http://proxys4all.cgi.net	- Information about proxy servers.
http://www.amazon.com	- Printed matter.
http://www.astalavista.com *	- Hackers/Crackers Search Engine.
http://www.bigfoot.com *	- Free Email and URL forwarding.
http://www.davecentral.com	- Programmer resources.

http://www.eff.com	- Electronic Frontier Foundation.
http://www.gutenberg.net *	- Home of free literature.
http://www.hotbot.com	- Search Engine, free webspace and email.
http://www.lycos.com	- Search Engine, free webspace and email.
http://www.thetutorial.com	- Various tutorials.
http://www.yahoo.com	- Search Engine, free webspace and email.

* *Highly Recommended*

Software

The software titles appearing in the list below have been suggested because they are reliable products with proven track records.

There are freeware/shareware products similar to the commercial ones in this list but they are not recommended, as they are not as secure or reliable.

A86	- Freeware Assembler.
Ameol *	- Freeware News/Email/Cix Reader.
AOL Instant Messenger	- Shareware Online/Offline messaging.
Borland C++ Compiler *	- Freeware C++ Compiler/Linker.
Borland Delphi	- Commercial *PASCAL* Programming.
Borland Turbo Assembler	- Commercial Programming (*TASM*).
Copernic 2000	- Shareware Multi Engine Searcher.
Cybersitter	- Shareware Censorship Software.
Eudora	- Freeware Newsreader.
Forté Agent	- Commercial Newsreader.
Forté Free Agent	- Freeware Newsreader.
Frontpage Express	- Freeware *HTML* Editor.
Ghost Mailer	- Freeware Anonymous Email Client.
ICQ	- Shareware Online/Offline messaging.

Info Disk	- Commercial Address, Phone No. Locator.
McAfee Anti-virus *	- Can't remember what this is?
McAfee Firewall	- Commercial Firewall.
Microsoft Macro Assembler	- Commercial Programming (*MASM*).
Microsoft Visual *BASIC*	- Commercial *BASIC* Programming.
mIRC	- Shareware Internet Relay Chat Client.
Musicmatch Jukebox	- Shareware *MP3* Player and Ripper.
Neoplanet *	- Freeware Browser and Email Client.
Nero Burning Rom	- Shareware CD Writing And Copying.
Netlab	- Freeware Tracing Tools.
Netnanny	- Shareware Censorship Software.
Netscape Communicator	- Freeware Browser, Email and *HTML* Editor.
Norton Anti-virus	- *Guess!*
Norton Ghost *	- Commercial Hard Drive Imaging Back-up.
Norton Utilities	- Commercial Utilities and Computer Tools.
Pklite	- Shareware Executable File Compressor.
Pkware Zip/Unzip	- Shareware Archiver.
Poco *	- Shareware Email Client.
The Cleaner	- Shareware Trojan Finder/Killer.
Winarj & Arj	- Shareware Archiver.
WinRar & Rar	- Shareware Archiver.
Winzip *	- Shareware Archiver.
Xnews	- Freeware Newsreader.
Yahoo Messenger	- Shareware Online/Offline messaging.
Zonealarm *	- Freeware Firewall.

** Highly Recommended*

About The Author

Bryan H. Joyce is a large, very non-stereotypical *Scotsman* who doesn't have red hair, a beard or wear a kilt. He is an experienced computer consultant, qualified tutor, and programmer. He loves all small fluffy animals and is scared of nothing except large animals, human beings and anything that looks, *"...a bit scary..."*

His forthcoming novel *"Jump On Zero"* has a main character called Bill Gates (no relation, just a coincidence) and is about cyber stalking (sort of). A short science fiction e-novel, *"The Tavern At The Edge Of Nowhere"*, is available as a free download on the World Wide Web. Where? From lots of different places, but you could try the originally titled www.bryanjoyce.co.uk first.

Bryan H. Joyce is of such an enormously substantial intellect that he does *not* need to refer to the instruction manual when using a toilet brush.

Starting and Running a Business on the Internet

Starting and Running a Business on The Internet offers realistic and practical advice for any existing business or budding 'Cyberpreneur'. It also:

- ❑ Helps you get started QUICKLY and CHEAPLY.
- ❑ Tells you which sites 'work', which don't and, WHY!
- ❑ Details how to PROMOTE your business online.
- ❑ Shows you how to stay ahead of your competitors.
- ❑ Warns you of the major PITFALLS and how to AVOID them.
- ❑ Highlights issues like CREDIT CARD handling and site SECURITY.

Alex Kiam 112 pages £6.95

The Net-Works Guide to
Marketing Your Website

Shows you how to construct and deliver a successful promotional strategy. It covers everything from the basics of linking to other sites and search engine registration, through to referral sales and associate programs. No stone is left unturned in the quest for more visitors. You will learn:

- How to promote your site in newsgroups and chat rooms without being flamed,
- The importance of META tags and how to use them,
- How to build customer loyalty,
- What is meant by 'sticky content' and how to write it,
- Why e-zines, newsletters and bait pages are important,
- Ways of promoting your site in the traditional media,

Tim Ireland 112 pages £7.95

The Internet for Managers

Many managers still view the Internet as a scary place. It appears to be the preserve of the technical wizard and even the acronyms seem incomprehensible. ***The Internet for Managers*** tackles this problem head on and gives all levels of management enough information to 'hold their own' in meetings and to take on board the issues which affect their spheres of responsibility. It explains all the key concepts from the basics of Web browsing through to the establishment of corporate security policies in clear, non-technical terms.

RRC Penfold 192 pages £12.95

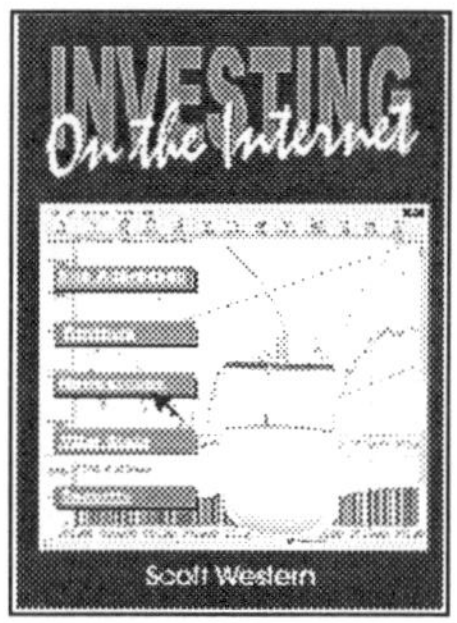

...on the Internet

Finding exactly what you want on the Internet is extremely difficult. There are several hundred million sites already in existence, and an estimated six million new pages are being added every week. Unfortunately there is no central repository for information and no catalogue of web sites. As a result, searching for the pages you want to view is a time consuming task, and frustrating when irrelevant pages and bad hits get in your way.
The ***... on the Internet*** series provides a detailed listing of the best sites in each category. Site addresses are given and all are reviewed in terms of content, layout and design, as well as the technical aspects such as speed of downloading, and ease of internal navigation.

Each title only £4.95

Book Ordering

To order any of these books, please order from our secure website at **www.net-works.co.uk** or complete the form below (or use a plain piece of paper) and send to:

Europe/Asia

TTL, PO Box 200, Harrogate HG1 2YR, England (or fax to 01423-526035, or email: sales@net-works.co.uk).

USA/Canada

Trafalgar Square, PO Box 257, Howe Hill Road, North Pomfret, Vermont 05053 (or fax to 802-457-1913, call toll free 800-423-4525, or email: tsquare@sover.net)

Postage and handling charge:

UK - £1 for first book, and 50p for each additional book

USA - $5 for first book, and $2 for each additional book (all shipments by UPS, please provide street address).

Elsewhere - £3 for first book, and £1.50 for each additional book via surface post (for airmail and courier rates, please fax or email for a price quote)

Book	Qty	Price
	Postage	
	Total:	

☐ I enclose payment for £______

☐ Please debit my VISA/AMEX/MASTERCARD

Number: ☐☐☐☐ ☐☐☐☐ ☐☐☐☐ ☐☐☐☐

Expiry Date: ☐☐☐☐ Signature: Date:

Name: ______________________________

Address: ______________________________

____

____

Postcode/Zip: ______________________________

Telephone/Email: ______________________________

scamsbk